Contents

Cut Your Texas Property Taxes

Patrick C.
O'Connor, MAI

ISBN: 1717466311
ISBN-13: 9781717466310

Acknowledgments

I am grateful for the constructive assistance of many persons who have made significant contributions to this book; to my wife, Kathleen, for her love, support and encouragement for more than 39 years; and to my mother, Lois O'Connor, who provided her encouragement throughout my life.

Preface

Cut Your Texas Property Taxes reveals the secrets of reducing your Texas property taxes for houses, commercial property and business personal property. If your primary interest is reducing property taxes for your home, you may want to start with Chapter 23 (page 279 - Quick Overview of Protesting Taxes for Your House). This chapter summarizes the steps and tasks involved. You can then read other chapters to increase your depth of knowledge on each topic.

This book approaches reducing your property taxes from a practical perspective. While theoretical issues are mentioned, the focus is on the mechanics of reducing your property taxes.

Anyone who wants to reduce his Texas property taxes can follow the steps presented in this book, whether the property is residential, commercial or business personal property. Exemptions and how to reduce assessed value are explained.

With the knowledge gained from this book, you can protest your taxes with confidence and with a good chance for success.

The author believes you can spend your money better than the government can.

Legal Disclaimer

The information contained in this text is for general guidance only. Given the changing nature of laws, rules, and regulations, there may be omissions or inaccuracies in information contained in this text. While we have attempted to ensure that the information contained in this text has been obtained from reliable sources, O'Connor is not responsible for any errors or omissions or for the results obtained from the use of this information. All information in this text is provided "as is," with no guarantee of the results obtained from the use of this information and without warranty of any kind, express or implied, including but not limited to warranties of performance, merchantability, and fitness for a particular purpose. In no event are O'Connor or employees thereof liable for any decision made or action taken in reliance on the information in this text or for any consequential, special, or similar damages, even if advised for the possibility of such damages.

Website addresses mentioned in this text referring to websites other than the O'Connor website are maintained by third parties over whom O'Connor has no control. O'Connor cannot attest to the accuracy or any other aspect of information contained in other websites.

Chapter 1: Yes, You Can Cut Your Property Taxes

You've received your annual notice from the local appraisal district. The appraised value of your property has gone up AGAIN! You know your property taxes are going to skyrocket.

WHAT CAN YOU DO?

This book will empower you to fight the appraisal district and lower your property taxes. We will look at many aspects of property taxes: how property taxes are calculated, how assessed values are set and, more importantly, what YOU can do to assure that you are paying the lowest possible property taxes. We will explain the possible exemptions and how to apply for them as well as take you, step by step, through the various types of protests and how to file a protest. You will learn how the property tax process works and the three approaches to performing an appraisal.

Finally, we will outline in detail the property tax protest hearing process so you will be ready to state your position and have the best possible opportunity to get your taxes lowered. You can do all this yourself or hire a professional to assist in some or all parts of the process.

Let's start by taking a quick look at the role of property taxes in funding governments so you will understand why there is little likelihood of property taxes being eliminated or assessed values lowered (without protest) by local taxing authorities.

THE ROLE OF PROPERTY TAXES IN FUNDING GOVERNMENT

Property taxes have traditionally been a major source of revenue for state and local governments. In Texas, property taxes are high compared to most other states, partly because Texas does not have a personal state income tax. Texas property taxes are used only to fund local government; they do not fund state government. At the local level, property taxes are used primarily to fund school districts, county government, city government, and municipal utility districts (MUDs). They are also assessed by a variety of other entities such as fire departments and community colleges.

The following table summarizes the percentage of property taxes as a funding source for various governmental entities in Texas:

PROPERTY TAX COMPARISON

Austin, Dallas, Houston, San Antonio

Entity	Tax Year	Total Budgeted Revenue ($000,000)	Budgeted Property Revenue ($000,000)	Property Taxes as % Of Total Revenue	Property Tax Rate %
Cities					
Austin	98-99	1522	167.4	11	0.5034
Dallas	98-99	1580.3	239.9	15.1	0.6675
Houston	98-99	1234	482.2	39.1	0.665
San Antonio	98-99	499.1	105	21.5	0.5798

Houston & San Antonio numbers reflect the
General Funds (primary section of city budget)

CITIES					
Austin	98-99	502.5	399.2	79.4	1.434
Dallas	98-99	823.8	552.9	67.1	1.46
Houston	98-99	1013.7	584	57.6	1.384
San Antonio	98-99	412.8	115.6	28	1.776

Chapter 1, Table 1

Property taxes have been–and are expected to continue to be–a significant component of revenue for local government in Texas, especially for local school districts.

In contrast, the state of Texas does not derive revenue from property taxes. The largest sources of revenue for the state of Texas are summarized in the following table:

LARGEST SOURCES OF REVENUE FOR STATE OF TEXAS 2015

Source	Amount (Millions)	% of Total
Federal Funds	50,992.56	32.7
Sales Tax	27,835.70	26.1
Licenses & Fees	34266.04	8.1
Other Revenue Sources	0.86	4.9
Corporation Franchise Tax	4,732.26	4.5
Motor Vehicle Taxes	4,209.95	4
Motor Fuels Tax	3,315.95	3.2
Net Lottery Proceeds	1,463.13	1.8
Interest Income	8,497.08	1.4
Insurance Company Taxes	1,947.90	1.9
Natural Gas Production Tax	1,899.58	1.8

Chapter 1, Table 2

Finally, property taxes in Texas are high compared to most other states due to the use of a personal income tax in other states. Texas does not have a state income tax. The following table (prepared by the Lincoln Institute of Land Policy and the Minnesota Center for Fiscal Excellence) summarizes effective tax rates (ETA) for 50 metropolitan areas:

4

LARGEST METROPOLITAN AREA MEDIAN VALUE HOMES

(Adjusted for differences in assessment practices)

(Personal property not included)

State/Metropolitan Area	2016 4thQuarter Median Home Prices	Net Tax	Effective Tax Rate %	ETR Rank
Alabama, Birmingham	93,000	621	0.668	48
Alaska, Anchorage	302,500	3,925	1.297	24
Arizona, Phoenix	200,800	1,926	0.959	37
Arkansas, Little Rock	162,000	1,802	1.112	32
California, Los Angeles	542,100	3,892	0.718	46
Colorado, Denver	316,700	1,971	0.623	50
Connecticut, Bridgeport	167,100	6,360	3.806	1
DC, Washington	551,300	3,936	0.714	47
Delaware, Wilmington	160,300	2,239	1.397	21

Florida, Jacksonville	146,500	1,347	0.92	38
Georgia, Atlanta	241,200	2,722	1.129	30
Hawaii, Honolulu	641,900	1,955	0.305	53
Idaho, Boise	209,900	1,687	0.804	43
Illinois, Aurora*	169,400	6,300	3.719	2
Illinois, Chicago	238,500	3,544	1.486	20
Indiana, Indianapolis	123,500	1,337	1.083	34
Iowa, Des Moines	119,500	2,748	2.3	6
Kansas, Wichita	124,400	1,513	1.216	27
Kentucky, Louisville	145,000	1,836	1.266	26
Louisiana, New Orleans	216,800	2,244	1.035	35
Maine, Portland	267,100	5,322	1.992	12
Maryland, Baltimore	155,600	3,247	2.087	9
Massachusetts, Boston	453,000	2,772	0.612	51
Michigan, Detroit	42,600	1,341	3.148	4
Minnesota, Minneapolis	227,500	3,171	1.394	22
Mississippi,	92,600	1,408	1.521	18

Jackson				
Missouri, Kansas City	138,400	2,066	1.493	19
Montana, Billings	208,200	1,792	0.861	41
Nebraska, Omaha	143,200	2,888	2.017	11
Nevada, Las Vegas	209,400	2,382	1.138	28
New Hampshire, Manchester	209,200	4,701	2.247	7
New Jersey, Newark	235,700	7,547	3.202	3
New Mexico, Albuquerque	189,200	2,409	1.273	25
New York, Buffalo*	75,800	1,494	1.971	13
New York, New York City	538,300	3,164	0.588	52
North Carolina, Charlotte	188,800	2,109	1.117	31
North Dakota, Fargo	192,400	1,882	0.978	36
Ohio, Columbus	137,100	2,803	2.044	10
Oklahoma, Oklahoma City	148,500	1,687	1.136	29
Oregon, Portland	348,300	5,614	1.612	17

Pennsylvania, Philadelphia	150,700	1,637	1.086	33
Rhode Island, Providence	177,400	3,036	1.712	16
South Carolina, Columbia	172,400	1,250	0.725	45
South Dakota, Sioux Falls	166,100	2,249	1.354	23
Tennessee, Memphis	94,400	1,735	1.837	14
Texas, Houston	**152,200**	**2,713**	**1.783**	**15**
Utah, Salt Lake City	262,400	2,165	0.825	42
Vermont, Burlington	282,800	6,044	2.137	8
Virginia, Virginia Beach	262,900	2,314	0.88	39
Washington, Seattle	530,900	4,658	0.877	40
West Virginia, Charleston	110,600	852	0.77	44
Wisconsin, Milwaukee	114,000	3,043	2.669	5
Wyoming, Cheyenne	204,500	1,324	0.648	49
Average	**221,785**	**2,768**	**1.439**	

*Anchorage, Alaska–Data from Assessor's Office, city specific.

*Wilmington, Delaware–Data from Assessor's Office, city specific.

*Jackson, Mississippi–Data from 1990 census adjusted for yearly growth of 5 %, city specific.

*Billings, Montana–Data from 1990 census, adjusted for yearly growth of 5%, city specific.

*Manchester, New Hampshire–Data from Assessor's Office, City specific.

*Philadelphia, Pennsylvania–1994 (metro-area) data from National Association of Realtors, adjusted to reflect the percent change for the *Northeast region from 1994 to 1997.

*Burlington, Vermont–Data from Assessor's Office, city specific.

*Seattle, Washington–3rd quarter, 1997 data from national Association of Realtors.

*Cheyenne, Wyoming–Data from 1990 census, adjusted for yearly growth of 5%, city specific.

Chapter 1, Table 3–Source: National Association of Realtors

For the taxpayer, the advantage of property taxes is that they can be protested and reduced in many cases. The disadvantage is that the tax continues regardless of the income of the property owner (or the property, if it is an income property). A property tax is in essence a first lien on the property held in perpetuity by the government.

For example, suppose a prosperous Texan owns a $1,000,000 house in an area with an aggregate 2.7% property tax rate. His annual property taxes would be $27,000 ($1,000,000 x 2.7%). During peak earning years, this may seem like a high but understandable level of taxation. However, if the homeowner's income is reduced or he retires, $27,000 per year may be a significant burden.

An income property owner faces a similar dilemma. Suppose the owner of a $10,000,000 class A office building pays property taxes of $270,000. While occupied, the taxes may be paid out of the revenues received from tenants. But if a major tenant leaves or the economy declines precipitously, the property taxes may decline slower than the income received by the owner. In this circumstance, property taxes can become an onerous burden.

 **PRACTICE TIP** – Decide to Pay Less Property Taxes

One way property owners may elect to reduce their property taxes is by reducing the value of their property. For example, a retired couple living in a $500,000 house could choose a more modest $150,000 house to reduce their annual property tax bill significantly. Assuming a three-percent tax rate and no homestead exemption, this would reduce their annual property taxes from $15,000 to $4,500.

Property taxes will continue to be a major component in funding local government in Texas for decades. This form of taxation is popular with governments because it is more stable than other types of taxes such as income or retail sales taxes. In addition, the government maintains a potent collection tool since it has a first lien on real estate if property taxes are not paid.

A constitutional amendment would be required to impose a state income tax. Without a dire financial crisis in funding local government, Texas voters will not amend the constitution to impose an income tax on themselves. Since an income tax is the only practical alternative to local property taxes, it is unlikely that property taxes will be abolished in Texas in the foreseeable future. Therefore, the Texas property owner's most effective options to reduce property taxes are to:

Understand how properties are valued,

and

Work diligently to reduce the assessed value of his property through the appeals process.

This book will review the property tax process and enable readers to make informed judgments about when to protest property taxes and how to do it, step by step. We'll start in the next chapter by looking at how property taxes are calculated.

O'Connor Tax Reduction Experts 713.369.5958

Special Offer to purchasers of

"Cut Your Texas Property Taxes"

Get a FREE evaluation to determine if you are being
overtaxed with our Texas Fairness Checker

Go to www.CutMyTaxes.com

Chapter 2: How Property Taxes Are Calculated

Texas property taxes are calculated using the following formula:

(Assessed Value-exemptions) x tax rate = Annual property tax

The central appraisal district (CAD) for each county in Texas sets the assessed value (AV) of real property. Some counties refer to a "county appraisal district" while others refer to a "central appraisal district." But they are the same in all but name. In Harris County, the Harris County Appraisal District (HCAD) sets the assessed value. *Exemptions are allowed for homestead status, veterans, homeowners over 65, and/or handicapped persons.* These are statutory tax benefits for homeowners established by the legislature and administered by the appraisal districts in each county. Tax entities have discretion over the level of exemption, and the level of exemption varies. Local tax entities also have latitude in allowing some tax exemptions such as "freeport," an exemption for taxes on inventory held for a limited time before being shipped outside the state. Finally, local tax entities also have discretion in the amount of homestead exemption they grant. Tax entities are also able to set limits on the growth of property taxes.

Tax rates are set by each taxing entity. These typically include school district, city and county. They may also include a municipal utility district (MUD), a community college, and a fire department (in a rural area).

The following example demonstrates how property taxes are calculated:

Market value for house (set by CAD)	$100,000
Homestead exemption	10,000
Handicapped exemption	5,000
Taxable amount	$85,000
Tax rate (for school district only) 1.6%	x.016
TOTAL SCHOOL TAXES	$1,360

The school district property taxes are as follows:

($100,000 - $10,000 - $5,000) x 1.6%

Or

$85,000 x 1.6% = $1,360

These are annual property taxes for the school district only. This process is repeated for each taxing entity. However, the same market value ($100,000 in this example) is used by each tax entity. Prior to 1980, each taxing entity set its own market value for each property.

Property taxes are paid annually in arrears, typically in December or January. Penalty and interest are added to the property taxes that are not paid by January 31 (for the previous year). There are typically 5 to 10 taxing entities per property, including the smaller ones, with one to three tax collectors serving them.

The three primary elements in calculating property taxes are:

> - **the market value set by the appraisal district, also known as the assessed value or the taxable value**
> - **exemptions, and**
> - **the tax rate**

Since the number and amount of the exemptions and the tax rate are set by government entities, property owners can only impact the assessed value. Reducing the assessed value can produce significant cuts in annual property taxes for the property owner **who understands and employs the property protest process.**

Texas property owners should become aware of and utilize all available exemptions. It is disappointing how many Texas homeowners do not utilize their homestead exemption. An analysis by O'Connor in January 2017 indicates nine percent of eligible Texas homeowners do not claim their homestead exemption. However, there is a limit as to how much progress can be made through the exemption process since this tax benefit is established by the legislature and the local tax entity.

Now that you know how property taxes are calculated, let's take a look at how the assessed value of your property is determined.

Chapter 3: Setting Assessed Value

In Texas, the central appraisal district in each county sets the proposed assessed value for over 19,154,000 properties. However, there are only 2,245 appraisers at the 250+ appraisal districts in Texas to value over 19 million properties! How many properties is that per appraiser each year? It works out to 8,463 appraisals per appraiser each year. This is a Herculean task for a limited staff and requires that appraisals be done en masse. The difference between *individual fee appraisal* and *mass appraisal* is significant and results in most Texas property owners paying excess property taxes.

FEE APPRAISAL VERSUS MASS APPRAISAL

During an individual fee appraisal, an appraiser visits the subject property, inspects comparables sales, and performs an analysis specifically for that property. Mass appraisal, as the name implies, is the process by which large volumes of properties are appraised - usually by an appraisal district trying to determine whether or how much to increase property values in an area. The *Uniform Standards of Professional Appraisal Practice*, 2015 edition, defines mass appraisal as follows: "The process of valuing a universe of properties as of a given date, utilizes standard methodology, employing common data and allowing for statistical testing."

The same source defines a mass appraisal model as "a mathematical expression of how supply and demand factors interact in a market." Thus, mass appraisal involves using: 1) information on your property, 2) a database with information on property sales, market income, market expenses, market vacancy and construction costs, and 3) a mathematical model to determine the assessed value for your property. **Obviously, the potential for error in the mass appraisal approach is significant.**

There are typically three or four errors in each mass appraisal: 1) the data for individual properties is not accurate, 2) the factors used to estimate replacement cost and similar factors are not accurate, 3) factors used to estimate depreciation are not accurate, and 4) the model used to calculate the value is not accurate. A good mass appraisal model will value half the properties between 90 and 110 percent of their actual value. About one-quarter of the properties will be valued at more than 110 percent of market value and one-quarter will be valued at less than 90 percent of market value.

WARNING! MASS APPRAISAL IS NOT RELIABLE!

Banks do not use appraisal district values for making real estate loans. They require fee appraisals prepared by state-licensed appraisers. Why you ask? Simple, because they like others involved in both commercial and residential real estate know the appraisal district values are not reliable. However, there seems to be a blind trust to government-computer generated numbers.

If the house was built prior to 1980, the appraisal district staff most likely has never seen the inside of the house. However, this does not limit their confidence in the accuracy data regarding the condition and grade of construction. (The grade of construction for property built prior to 1980 was likely estimated by one of the tax entities and then merged into a larger database after the appraisal districts were founded in 1980/1981.)

If your property was built after 1980, the appraisal district probably inspected and measured your property when it was built. This function is often performed by entry-level appraisers and is part of the training process for new appraisers. For example, in one large appraiser district, entry level appraisers are instructed to measure the house to the nearest foot when sketching and measuring the property. A series of rounding errors to the nearest foot may serve either to understate or overstate the actual size of the property. The appraiser also makes judgments as to quality of construction, the class of building, the grade of building materials, and other subjective factors when inspecting during the construction stage.

Appraisal districts often have fifteen to twenty grades of construction, which creates an artificial sense of accuracy. Fee appraisers valuing houses use a system that has six grades. In practice, it is often difficult to differentiate between grades. Fannie Mae has written criteria and a system termed "Collateral Underwriter" to ensure consistency with only six grades of construction. The grade of construction includes factors such as the elevation, exterior building materials, portion of the house with windows and the quality of finish. Appraisal districts really believe they can differentiate between fifteen to twenty levels of grade and use this system to value property. While fee appraisers are often in the business for an entire career and become experts at selecting one of the six levels of grade, at many appraisal districts, entry level appraisers who inspect new houses have a high turnover rate, further undermining the quality of their data.

PROPERTY INFORMATION TRACKED BY THE APPRAISAL DISTRICT

As stated above, the appraisal district will typically use aerial photography to update their records on grade, condition, level of remodel and effective year of construction every five to seven years. (It may be more frequent in smaller counties with a limited number of properties.) You may wonder how the appraisal districts are able to only "inspect" property every five to seven years when the statutes require inspections every three years. In practice, appraisal districts select the statutes they will follow and ignore the balance.

21

This is one of the weak points in the Texas property tax system. There is no effective check and balance when appraisal districts knowingly ignore the law. There are many and varied examples of appraisal districts and appraisal review boards ignoring statutes. These will be addressed by section along with suggestions for legislative remedies when appropriate.

The limited level of inspection performed by the appraisal district is mostly a consequence of budgetary constraints. In fairness to appraisal districts, they do not choose to limit the accuracy of their data regarding property; they simply do not have resources to maintain high-quality data for most property. Further, it would be invasive for the appraisal district physically to inspect every property every year. The result is that CAD appraisal records are not accurate for your property, either overstating or understating quality and size factors, resulting in an overstatement or understatement of the assessed value. Given the large number of fields of data tracked by the appraisal districts for each property, they rarely have completely accurate information for any property.

Databases regarding property and property valuation factors are the heart of the mass appraisal process. Appraisal districts mostly compile information on all properties within the county. They outsource valuation and gathering property data for limited exceptions, such as industrial property (refineries) and mineral producing properties. Appraisal districts devote substantial resources gathering information on construction costs and comparable sales.

The Harris County Appraisal District tracks the following field data for residential properties:

PROPERTY RECORD DOCUMENT

PRD–Explanation of Terms:

NAME & ADDRESS–The property owner's name and mailing address

SITUS ADDRESS–The location address for this parcel

TAX YEAR–The year of record being complied, i.e., 1999

ACCOUNT NUMBERS–Corresponding account numbers for this parcel

SALES DATA–Sales information on the property , if any exists

PID–The parcel identification number

CLASS–The property class, i.e., whether the parcel is residential, commercial, apartment, etc.

USE–The land use code of the parcel

NEIGHBORHOOD–The neighborhood assigned to this parcel by this modeling group

LIVING UNITS–The number of living units (i.e., single family, duplex, etc.) on this property

ZONING–The key map page and letter where this property is located

LEGAL DESCRIPTION–The legal description for the year in question

PARCEL TIEBACK–The PID for a related parcel (if applicable)

PSF–The parcel status flag for this parcel

DESCRIPTOR–This area describes the use of the parcel; in this case IMPR (improved)

OWNERSHIP–The type of ownership

PROPERTY FACTORS–Some general information about the property site

CONDOMINIUM–Special information concerning condominiums

LAND DATA/COMPUTATIONS–Land information and at the far right any land influences (factors which positively or negatively affect the value of the land)

FIELD NOTES–The field notes

TOTAL ACRES–The total land size of all entries expressed in acres

GROSS IAND–The gross land value, if any; may be either positive or negative

TOTAL VALUE–The total value of the land

BUILDING DESCRIPTION/COMPUTATIONS–This describes some of the building's physical features and the cost approach to value. It addresses style, exterior wall, year built, year remodeled, foundation, heating/cooling, attic, rooms, cost factor, replacement cost new (estimated cost to build the improvements), quality, percentage depreciation, value of out buildings, and cost approach market value.

ADDITIONS–Those items, called additions, attached to the main part of house. The letter used under "no" relates to the letter on the sketch. Items cataloged include number of bathrooms, number of half bathrooms, condition, fireplaces, number of stories, base area, cost, additions, and grade/quality.

OTHER BLDG & YARD IMPROVEMENTS–Those items not attached to the house, but on the parcel in question

SKETCH–A computer drawing based on information gathered in the field

BUILDING AREA–The total square feet of living area in the house. This DOES NOT include the areas of garages, porches, AC area, etc.

RCN/LA (Replacement Cost New/Living Area)–The result when replacement cost new is divided by living area and expressed as dollars per square foot of living area

APPRAISAL–The value placed on the property for the current year

CURRENT ASSESSED VALUES–Current year's land and improvement assessed values

PREVIOUS ASSESSED VALUE–Previous year's land and improvement assessed values

OTHER FEATURES–Other features considered include atrium, lower-level garage, lower-level recreation room, lower-level living area, and unfinished area

LAND DATA–Influencing factors in the land data computations include size, topography, flood zone, corner, view, alley shape, nonconforming improvements, etc.

PROPERTY FACTORS–Besides topography, the following factors are also considered: types of utilities, type of street, parking, and adjoining properties

A sample HCAD record card for a residential property is shown on the following page.

THIS DOCUMENT CONTAINS CONFIDENTIAL INFORMATION
2017 APPRAISAL EVIDENCE SUMMARY

Official Government Document
Provided by the
Harris County Appraisal District

Property Location

Additional Information

New Owner Date	7/12/1989
Exemptions	Residential Homestead
Acreage	0.1742 AC
Land Area	7,590 SF
Land / SF	$33.13
Tiebacks Exist	No
Undivided Interest Account	No
Evidence Requested (as of 5/1/2017)	No

Building Characteristics

A1 -- Real, Residential, Single-Family	
A1 -- Real, Residential, Single-Family	
1001 -- Residential Single Family	
Number of Bldgs	1
Building % Complete (Bldg 1)	100%
Year Built / Remodeled	1962 / 0
Effective Year Built	1962
Total Base Area (All Bldgs)	1,498
Total Bedrooms (All Bldgs)	3
Total Baths: Full / Half (All Bldgs)	2 / 0
Cond. / Desir. / Util. (CDU)	Good
Grade	C+
Foundation Type	Slab
Exterior Wall	Brick / Veneer
Cost and Design	None

Recent Sales Information *

There are no recorded sales for this property in tax years 2014 - 2017.

Extra Features

#	Description	Units
1	Canopy - Residential	1

Primary Valuation Method: Reconcile

Noticed Value Detail

Total Improvement Value	$68,570
Land Value	$251,430
Market Value	$320,000
Appraised Value	$320,000
New Construction Value	$0

Equity Analysis

Subject Value At Median:	$347,800

Improved Sales Transactions *

0925300000004 08/10/2006

#	Sale Date	Grade	Living Area	Address	Year Built	Cost and Design	Src	Vld	Sale Price	Time Adj Sale Price	Final Adj Sale Price

REFER TO THE TRANSACTION REPORT AND SUPPLEMENTAL EVIDENCE FOR SALES INFORMATION

* The list above contains information that is confidential under Sec. 552.115, Government Code. Neither the property owner nor an owner's agent may disclose this information to third parties. The information may not be used for any purpose except as evidence of an argument of the hearing on the protest for which the information was provided.

* The Harris County Appraisal District plans to introduce information available through Google Maps and Google Earth, including but not limited to, maps, satellite imagery, street view photography, geographical and topographical detail, and webcam images. These items may be accessed on the internet or in our information center using Google coverage.

27

Harris County Appraisal District tracks the following fields of data for commercial properties: type of lot, size of primary and secondary site, likely use of lot, other details affecting the site (shape, topography, corner, view, etc.), parking, street frontage, type of building, and construction details for the building (frame, foundation, exterior walls, heating/cooling, sprinkler, plumbing, condition, functional utility, on-site parking, canopy, etc.).

A sample HCAD record card for a commercial property is shown on the following page.

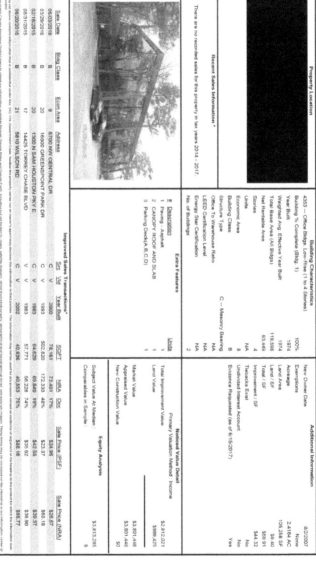

THIS DOCUMENT CONTAINS CONFIDENTIAL INFORMATION
2017 APPRAISAL EVIDENCE SUMMARY

Property Location

Recent Sales Information *

There are no recorded sales for this property in tax years 2014 - 2017.

Building Characteristics

4353 — Office Bldg. Low-Rise (1 to 4 Stories)	
Building % Complete (Bldg. 1)	100%
Year Built	1974
Weighted Avg. Effective Year Built	1974
Total Base Area (All Bldgs)	119,598
Net Rentable Area	63,449
Stories	4
Units	NA
Economic Area	8
Building Class	B
Structure Type	C — Masonry Bearing
Office To Warehouse Ratio	NA
LEED Certification Level	NA
Energy Star Certification	NA
No. of Buildings	2

Extra Features

#	Description	Units
1	Paving - Asphalt	1
2	CANOPY ROOF AND SLAB	1
3	Parking Deck(A,B,C,D)	1

Additional Information

New Owner Date	8/2/2007
Exemptions	None
Acreage	2.4164 AC
Land Area	105,256 SF
Land / SF	$9.40
Total / SF	$59.91
Improvement / SF	$44.32
Tiebacks Exist	No
Undivided Interest Account	No
Evidence Requested (as of 6/15/2017)	Yes

Noticed Value Detail

Primary Valuation Method: Income

Total Improvement Value	$2,812,021
Land Value	$989,425
Market Value	$3,801,446
Appraised Value	$3,801,446
New Construction Value	$0

Equity Analysis

Subject Value At Median :	$3,813,285
Comparables in Sample :	9

Improved Sales Transactions *

#	Sale Date	Bldg Class	Econ Area	Address	Src	Vid	Year Built	SQFT	NRA	Occ	Sale Price (PSF)	Sale Price (NRA)
1	06/03/2016	B	9	5700 NW CENTRAL DR	C	V	2000	78,161	73,401	17%	$24.95	$26.57
2	03/29/2016	B	20	16800 GREENSPOINT PARK DR	C	V	1993	502,820	172,333	48%	$23.37	$68.18
3	02/18/2015	B	20	1300 N SAM HOUSTON PKY E	C	V	1983	64,629	60,849	19%	$42.55	$39.37
4	08/31/2015	B	17	14425 TORREY CHASE BLVD	V	V	1983	57,771	56,228	74%	$35.62	$36.90
5	06/20/2016	B	21	5810 WILSON RD	C	V	2002	40,836	40,553	75%	$88.16	$88.77

Based on the large number of fields of data (more than 50) and the 1.6 million properties for which Harris County Appraisal District tracks information, *it is maintaining more than 42 million fields of data!* It is inconceivable that all the information will be accurate; however, most of the information is accurate for most of the properties.

 PRACTICE TIP - Inaccurate data on the record card is one option for protesting property taxes.

Special Offer to purchasers of

"Cut Your Texas Property Taxes"

Get a FREE evaluation to determine if you are being overtaxed with our Texas Fairness Checker

Go to www.CutMyTaxes.com

INCONSISTENT PRACTICES IN APPRAISAL DISTRICTS

No Consistent Standards with Appraisal Districts

Appraisal District Attitudes: ☺

☹☺☹☺☹☺☹☺☹☺☹☺☹☺☹☺☹☺☹☺☹☺☹☺☹

There are over 250 appraisal districts in Texas, and each one is a privately run fiefdom. What the chief appraiser says goes, regardless of the Tax Code. Many appraisal districts make every effort to generously resolve disputes in the favor of the property owner because they realize the limits to the accuracy of their valuations. Other appraisal districts consider protests akin to an assault on their honor. They are incredulous if the property owner suggests that the appraisal district may have made a mistake.

 PRACTICE TIP – Appraisal districts are not like McDonald's restaurant; each one is different.

Most appraisal districts make an effort to extend property owners every courtesy, provided their request is legitimate and legal. Other appraisal districts place artificial limitations on settlements by their staff. For example, at Harris County Appraisal District (HCAD), it is quite unusual to get an informal agreement to settle a residential account with a reduction in excess of $100,000 or more.

Our team reports that there are about 20 informal settlements with a reduction over $100,000 in over 2 million hearings, that is one in 100,000.

The point is not to pick on HCAD. However, this is the type of issue that causes appeals to continue to binding arbitration or the judicial appeal phase. By not allowing appraisers to exercise judgment for accounts with a change in excess of $100,000, HCAD essentially provides owners of larger homes two choices: 1) accept whatever value is proposed by the appraisal review board or 2) file for binding arbitration. This policy encourages annual appeals of homes with a certain value threshold and higher. Conversely, the luxury homes are resolved as part of the appeal process for more counties.

IMPACT OF ARTIFICIAL LIMITS ON ARGUMENTS OR EVIDENCE CONSIDERED

There are two separate issues here: 1) does an appraisal district and/or an appraisal review board considers unequal appraisal and 2) are there artificial requirements regarding evidence or settlement. Let's take these in order?

Many appraisal districts no longer personally inspect the property they are assessing. Texas law requires appraisal districts to "inspect" each parcel of real property at least once every three years. However, the inspection can be done using aerial photography. Further, based on handling over a million HCAD appeals, it appears they typically "inspect" properties every five to seven years, most using aerial photography. The inspections done with aerial photography clearly undermine the accuracy of the appraisal district's data. However, while the limitations are clear to outsiders, appraisal districts typically take the position that their information is indisputable unless the property owner brings extensive documentation. It can almost be comical. If the property owner brings photographs, he may be asked for bids for the cost of repairs. If the property owner brings bids, they are asked for photographs. When a property owner brings bids and photographs, the deferred maintenance is sometimes considered "routine maintenance," such as the cost to replace a roof or HVAC.

APPRAISAL DISTRICTS AND APPRAISAL REVIEW BOARDS ARE NOT CONSIDERING UNEQUAL APPRAISAL

The two primary bases for appeal of property taxes in Texas include value over market and property unequally appraised. However, the practice of the vast majority of appraisal districts and appraisal review boards is to ignore evidence on unequal appraisal. It is impossible to explain how appraisal review boards, theoretically independent, rule in favor of the appraisal district over 99% of the time on unequal appraisal.

THE PROBLEM WITH APPRAISAL REVIEW BOARDS

Appraisal Review Boards are supposed to be citizen boards set up to hear disputes the property owner and appraisal district were unable to resolve in the informal hearing. The appraisal review boards are supposed to be impartial and independent, though paid by the appraisal district. The law requires they vote in favor of the property owner, unless the appraisal district proves their case by a preponderance of the evidence.

EXPLAIN HOW THE APPRAISAL DISTRICT WINS WITH NO EVIDENCE

When both parties present evidence, it is impossible to accurately know the thought process of the finder of fact, the appraisal review board (ARB). But what happens when the appraisal district has no evidence? Keep in mind that Texas appraisal review boards are required by law to vote in favor of the property owner, unless the appraisal district prevails by a preponderance of the evidence presented at the hearing. ARB members take an oath. This applies to both market value and unequal appraisal. (Tax Code 41.43)

However, in thirty or so hearings attended by the author, when the appraisal district had no evidence, the appraisal review board still voted with the appraisal district in about 28 to 30 cases. When appraisal review boards vote against the property owner over 90% of the time, it clearly reveals the bias to the appraisal district.

Chapter 4: Why Do So Few People Protest Their Property Taxes?

For reasons not clear to me, only a tiny fraction of property owners appeal their property taxes. Consider the following:

Total property tax parcels in Texas:	19,207,001
Total number of tax protests	1,579,386 (8%)
Informal protests	923,246
Successful informal protests	636,273 (69%)
Formal Protests	338,630
Successful formal protests	173,164 (51%)
People who filed a protest but did not attend the hearing	317,510 (20%)
Lawsuits	10,716
Binding Arbitrations	11,102

O'Connor Tax Reduction Experts 713.369.5958

2016 Texas Comptroller Study of Appraisal Districts

WHY DO ONLY 8% OF PROPERTY OWNERS PROTEST?

What is amazing to the writer is that while 69% of informal protests and 51% of formal property tax protests are successful, only 8% of property owners bother to file a property tax protest. In case it is not clear, the data shown above was sourced from the Texas Comptroller for the tax year 2016 which is the most recent year available. The numbers shown above are after we cleaned the Texas Comptroller's data errors.

There are many reasons to file a property tax protest and few reasons not to file. It is surprising to the author that more people do not protest. Consider the following:

You must file a property tax protest to obtain the appraisal district's evidence package, including comparable sales data and unequal appraisal.

In many cases, the appraisal district's evidence package contains information to support a reduction; remember 69% of accounts with a hearing got a reduction.

Appraisal districts are inclined to resolve appeals, preferably at the informal level. In the Texas Comptroller data from 2015, there were 790,158 informal settlements versus 301,330 formal (appraisal review board appeals). In other words, more than two appeals were settled informally for every appeal that had a formal hearing, and still 69% of those receive a reduction.

You are helping your neighbors and your community by protesting. More protests mean that the appraisal district staff is motivated to resolve appeals quickly!

You are 1) improving the economy by diverting funds from the government to the private sector, 2) defending your property against unlawful government taxation, and 3) asserting your right as a citizen.

 PRACTICE TIP - Be a patriot! Be part of the solution! Stand up for your rights; be sure to protest your property taxes annually.

DO HOMEOWNERS GET A FAIR DEAL ON PROPERTY TAXES IN TEXAS?

Owners of commercial property and large residential

properties routinely file a judicial appeal and obtain another 10% or so reduction, below what was achieved at the appraisal review board hearing. A judicial appeal requires filing fees of about $400 (nonrefundable) and hiring an attorney or just hiring a tax consulting firm to coordinate the process.

Binding arbitration is an option for owners of smaller properties. It does not require an attorney or an expert witness. The finder of fact (arbitrator) is typically a real estate agent, but appraisers and attorneys also do binding arbitration hearings.

Let's consider a 10% value error for a $200,000 house. It is valued at $220,000 but should be valued at $200,000. Should the owner file for binding arbitration? On the positive side, if they are successful, the tax savings would be about $540, assuming a 2.7% tax rate. On the other hand, the property owner has to put up a deposit of $450 for the arbitration. If they win (arbitrator's value is $1 closer to their value than ARB value), the appraisal district pays the $400 arbitrator fee. (The Texas Comptroller retains $50 as a processing fee.) However, assume the value is reduced to $210,000; the property owner benefits from about a $270 tax savings but does not get back any of the $450 deposit. The taxpayer has a loss of $180.

However, assume the home value is $1,000,000 and the

assessed (tax) value is $1,100,000. Let's again assume a split-the-difference decision (final value of $1,050,000) and see how it works for the property owner.

Tax savings - $50,000 x 2.7% = $1,350

Fee not refunded - 500 (fee is higher for houses over $500,000)

Net tax savings - 850

So while the owner of a $200,000 home lost $180 on a binding arbitration hearing with a 5% reduction, the owner of a $1,000,000 home gained $850 in identical circumstances.

CONCLUSION

Savvy owners of larger homes and commercial properties routinely utilize all levels of the property tax appeal process, including binding arbitration and judicial appeals as the circumstances require. (Note: while filing property tax appeals in the State Office of Administrative Hearings (SOAH) is possible, the number of filings relative to the volume of judicial appeals and binding arbitration is nominal; only 59 in 2016.) Commercial property owners fair better since they can and do appeal more aggressively.

THE THREE APPROACHES TO VALUING REAL ESTATE

For well over 100 years, a relatively small amount of time relative to the history of man, valuation of real estate has focused exclusively on three approaches: 1) cost approach, 2) sales comparison approach and 3) income approach.

Appraisers look through the eyes of market participants to estimate value. This makes sense. If you are trying to value something, you study how the buyers and sellers are pricing. The cost approach is primarily of benefit for new buildings, but even then may not be the most relevant approach. The sales comparison approach is used almost exclusively for homes and for owner-occupied real estate where the income approach is not relevant. The income approach is most relevant for income property. Buyers and sellers of income property would value based on the income approach. Following is a brief summary of the three methods and their advantages and disadvantages.

COST DATA

Cost data is typically purchased by the CAD from outside sources to monitor and calculate replacement cost. Replacement cost as defined by the *Dictionary of Real Estate Appraisal, 6th edition*, which is the most recent edition published by the Appraisal Institute, states, "The estimated cost to construct, at current prices as of the effective date, a building with utility equivalent to the building being appraised, using modern materials and current standards, design and layout."

Construction cost data is typically purchased from national vendors such as Marshall & Swift or RSMeans. These firms track construction costs on a national basis and use a combination of base cost, regional multipliers, and local cost multipliers to estimate the construction costs for hundreds of property types and classes of property across the country. While the costs are often good indicators of the actual construction costs, they are not accurate since costs change more quickly than can be reported. Further, errors in the grade and condition of property record cards maintained by the appraisal district further limit the accuracy. *The bottom line is that the accuracy of the cost estimate depends on the quality of the subject property information AND the accuracy of the cost data.*

COMPARABLE SALES DATA

Comparable sales data is an important component of the mass appraisal system. Over 250 separate Texas appraisal districts gather data from a variety of sources for property sales in the county, including both residential and commercial sales for a variety of geographic areas. The following is a partial summary of the fields of data compiled by the Harris County Appraisal District for residential sales:

THE SALES REPORT REFERENCE SHEET

HEADER: The header line of the report contains the Tax Year of the report; the ISD CODE, the NEIGHBORHOOD NUMBER, and the NEIGHBORHOOD GROUP NUMBER.

1) **NO.**–The sequence of items listed on this report

2) **ACCOUNT NUMBER**–The HCAD account number for this item

3) **LUC**–The LAND USE CODE for this parcel

4) **SALE DATE**–The date the parcel was sold or rental data acquired

5) **SALES CODES**–The type of transaction

TRANS AMOUNT–The price for which the property was sold or the rental amount, expressed in dollars. An "x" means special attention is called to type, source, and validity codes.

LAND SQ FT VALUE–The size of the land, expressed in square feet, and the land value for the current year

PAR T/B–A "yes" symbol indicates more than one parcel is involved; left blank if no tie-back (related property tax account which is part of the same economic unit) is known

STY HGT–Number of stories within the building

YEAR BLT/RM–The year in which the building was constructed, year remodeled, if applicable

GRADE–Grade of construction for the building; relates to grade of materials used

CDU–Condition, Desirability & Utility

TOTAL SFLA–Total square footage living area (heated & cooled)

OB &Y* TYPE VALUE–

CODES:

P–pool

G–garage

C–carport

T–tennis

0–other

S–series

Dollar amount indicates the value attributed to the OB&Y which is included in the improvement value.

Sales data is collected from sources such as MLS (Multiple Listing Service), data presented at hearings, questionnaires sent to property buyers and sellers, and phone calls to buyers and sellers. There are reasonable and appropriate methods of collecting data. However, there are multiple opportunities for inaccurate data to be included in the database, including data entry errors by the real estate agent typing the MLS sales data, intentional errors by property owners not wishing to disclose accurate information on their property, and inadvertent errors by buyers and sellers who did not correctly remember the sales price for a property.

Even more important than errors in the reported sales price is information regarding the condition of the property sold and the allocation of the sales price between real estate and **intangibles.** Real estate is land and physical improvements to the land. Intangibles include contracts, guarantees, promises to pay a set level of rent, agreements to repair property, cash set aside at closing for repairs, and many other factors. While intangibles are more typically a factor in commercial real estate transactions, there are opportunities to include intangibles in the sale of a house. For example, if a rental house is sold, a guarantee by the seller that the buyer will receive a set amount of monthly income for a set period of time would be an intangible. Any personal property left by the seller should not be included in the sales price for the real estate. The buyer and seller could agree to an allocation of real estate and personal property. There are a variety of options to reduce the portion of consideration allocated to real estate. Having a lower amount allocated to real estate would probably reduce the property taxes for the purchaser for the first several years of ownership.

Suggestion:

Include a nondisclosure clause in your contract when *buying* a property to ensure that the purchase price is not released to the appraisal district. The sales price (if available to the appraisal district) will probably be used to establish your assessed value if the property was purchased recently. Since many properties are assessed at less than market value, it is likely the sales price will be higher than the assessed value at the time of the sale. Adjusting the sales value to the purchase price will probably result in an increase in assessed value and property taxes. Hence, it is advantageous to release the sales price to the appraisal district only if the property is assessed for more than the sales price.

 PRACTICE TIP – In some cases it may pay to obtain an appraisal of the real estate and the intangible personal property and have only the real estate included on the closing statement.

Sales processed through the MLS will typically be utilized by appraisal districts in their database to assess value. Unless prohibited, the sales price of your private transaction becomes public information. Unfortunately, it is difficult to not disclose sales prices for property sold through the MLS.

The mass appraisal process is used to calculate the value unless it is overridden by a transaction price from a recent sale. **The three primary methods of appraising real estate include the cost, income, and the sales comparison approaches.** The following is a brief summary of these three approaches.

COST APPROACH

Replacement cost of the building when new

Less depreciation (all types)

Plus market value of the land

Equals the value of the property

The cost approach starts with an estimate of replacement cost. Depreciation is subtracted from the replacement cost for items such as physical deterioration, functional obsolescence, and economic obsolescence. From a practical perspective, the only type of depreciation tracked by most appraisal districts is physical depreciation because it is difficult to properly calculate depreciation from other causes with a limited level of inspection of the property.

Appraisal districts typically use the cost approach to value houses and commercial property other than income producing property. Except for relatively new property, the cost approach is generally considered the least reliable approach to value. Appraisers performing valuations for financial institutions either do not use the cost approach or they may include it because it is required. However, unless the property is less than five to ten years old, the cost approach is given almost no consideration for commercial property. The cost approach is given even less consideration for houses. Single-family appraisers include it if they are required to do so but give it little to no consideration.

 PRACTICE TIP – Appraisal districts are not typically aware of function or exterior obsolescence.

The dichotomy of valuation methodology between appraisal districts and professional appraisers performing valuations for financial institutions deserves consideration. The reality is that the appraisal districts have no practical option other than the cost approach given the volume of property they must value. However, using the cost approach generates the least reliable value. Use of the cost approach by appraisal districts explains why their estimates of value are off by more than 10 percent more than half the time.

The volume of property tax protests would likely be much higher if property owners understood the following: 1) the cost approach generates unreliable results, 2) there is only one chance in two that the appraisal district's value for their property is within ten percent of the actual value, and 3) they can protest on unequal appraisal.

Appraisal districts use the cost approach to value all property except land.

INCOME APPROACH

The income approach to value is based on the premise that investors buy income properties for the income stream. The income approach converts an estimate of the net income for the real estate to an estimate of market value using a conversion factor. The conversion factor is typically either a capitalization rate or a gross income multiplier.

There are a number of steps involved in performing the income approach and an error in any of them erodes the accuracy of the estimate of value. Multiple errors in estimating multiple components of the income approach render the result unreliable. Appraisers perform the income approach by estimating the gross (total) potential revenue a property should be able to achieve. Vacancy and operating expenses are deducted to calculate net operating income. Net operating income is converted to an indication of market value using a capitalization rate. The income approach can also be utilized based on a gross revenue multiplier (GRM), an effective gross income multiplier (EGIM), or a discounted cash flow analysis. The income approach is not typically used to value single-family homes or land.

SALES COMPARISON APPROACH

The sales comparison approach is based on the premise that similar properties will sell for a similar price. By comparing recent sales of property, similar to the subject property an appraiser can estimate what a purchaser is likely to pay for the subject property by making adjustments for difference between the subject property and comparable sales. *This is the method used typically to value single-family homes.* It is also used extensively in the valuation of most types of commercial properties. Intangibles should be excluded from the stated purchase price or separated in a summary.

The limited appraisal staff at the major central appraisal districts must appraise a very large number of properties. Consider the following summary showing the number of appraisals per appraiser/employee at major appraisal districts:

NUMBER OF APPRAISALS PER EMPLOYEE AT LARGE CADS

County	Number of Certified Appraisers	Number of Properties	Appraisals Per Employee Per Year (Appraiser)	Appraisals Per Workday(1)
Harris	280	1,623,452	7,000	29.2
Dallas	87	828,387	4,639	19.3
Tarrant	92	1,253,653	9,958	41.5
Travis	61	423,981	12,185	50.8
Ft. Bend	40	339,581	11,474	47.8
Montgomery	41	296,169	9,153	38.1
Galveston	16	189,230	12,401	51.7
Waller	6	41,190	15,458	64.4
Bexar	77	671,267		

(1) Based on 240 workdays per year, for 1998 or 1999

Chapter 4, Table 1

OPPORTUNITIES FOR ERRORS

There are many opportunities for errors in the mass appraisal process. A series of small errors or one significant error can result in an incorrect assessed value for your property. The following are some examples of the types of errors which typically occur:

The appraiser performing the construction inspection of your property can make errors, including measurements of size and judgments regarding the quality of construction and construction materials. Subsequent inspection may not accurately judge the effective age of your property or the existence of functional obsolescence.

The appraisal district does not have accurate information on your building. It may or may not be close. There are too many parcels and too few tax assessors to accurately value real estate effective January 1.

The author recently attended an International Association of Assessment Officers convention as a speaker. The content in other sessions was most amazing. For example, it is clear the while the value of many leased stores is in the credit of the guarantor of the lease, appraisal districts are not giving any consideration to this guarantee. Their position is that there is no difference in value between a building leased to Walgreens and an individual local tenant.

Fraud detection audits in 2017 are catching legitimate home owners in their snare. HCAD has apparently concluded there are a meaningful number of fraudulent homestead exemptions. However, in a case where the author has personal knowledge, a widow received a notice that they were cancelling her homestead and over-65 exemption. Fortunately, she had the spirit to challenge. The home was titled in her deceased husband's name. Since he is dead and the house is still titled in his name, they apparently assumed it was fraud.

HCAD appraisers measure buildings to the nearest foot in length. In most cases, this works. However, in some cases, each length seems to be x feet and 7 inches.

There are over 100 fields of data for a single property at most appraisal districts. Many appraisal districts are not able to visit the properties.

Errors in a single field of data, such as land value per square foot, effective age, construction grade or condition can cause a home to be overvalued by 20% to 50%.

Errors with comparable sales can include items such as the sales price, the size of the subject property, the quality (a Class B office building versus a Class C office building), and its rental or occupancy rate.

Cost data provided by a national service may or may not be accurate for your property type in your city. If you have an atypical property, there may be insufficient data to perform a regression analysis. For example, there may be insufficient data to perform a mass appraisal of a specialized manufacturing facility.

When valuing property after a natural disaster some appraisal districts and appraisal review boards become confused between real estate and intangible personal property. In many cases, appraisal district staff and appraisal review board staff have taken the position that if you have insurance, the value of severely damaged property should not be considered. However, this is simply wrong. The relevant issue is the market value of the real estate on January 1 of the tax year in question.

Some appraisal districts do not apply a discount for diminution of value due to flooding after a natural disaster. They assume the only reduction in value is for the cost to rebuild and do not include the discount for having to disclose flooding and the 15 risks of rebuilding. This misguided and unlawful approach is estimated to cost Gulf Coast residents over $2 billion in 2018.

Some appraisal districts have not been receptive to factor in business enterprise value (BEV) which is a factor in the value of commercial hotel, self-storage, hospitals, restaurants and other type of commercial real estate.

While the market value of real estate is subject to the ad valorem (based on value) tax, the value of a business is not subject to the ad valorem tax. This is a source of controversy for properties such as **hotels, hospitals, restaurants, apartments, self-storage,** and **nursing homes** which involve a combination of business and real estate. For example, a nursing home may sell for a price which is much higher than the construction cost of real estate. The appraisal principal of **substitution** states that a property will not sell for more than the cost of replacing it. Since nursing homes often sell for more than the cost to build the real estate, the value of the operating business including items such as an established clientele, a trained and coordinated staff, and a license for the facility. The mass appraisal process may not segregate the real estate value from any business enterprise value (BEV). Using sales of nursing homes to estimate the market value of the real estate for a nursing home facility may inadvertently result in including the business enterprise value in addition to the estate value.

***

In summary, mass appraisal is a reasonable and appropriate methodology for valuing large numbers of properties with a limited staff. One of the consequences of utilizing mass appraisal, however, is that errors will result from factors such as inaccurate property records or comparable sales, errors in judgment in developing the appraisal valuation model, inadequate data to perform a mass appraisal, and combining the market value of the real estate with the business enterprise value. *These mass appraisal limitations provide many opportunities to reduce your property taxes.*

Chapter 5: Exemptions From Property Taxes

Taking advantage of all available exemptions is the quickest and easiest way to lower your property taxes. In this chapter we shall look at the various exemptions, who is eligible, and how to apply for them.

RESIDENTIAL HOMESTEAD EXEMPTION

The residential homestead exemption is available to Texas homeowners for their principle residence. This is the most common type of property tax exemption in Texas and can be obtained by completing the form on the following page and returning it to your central appraisal district. Your local CAD can provide a copy of the form and answer questions on preparing it. *You can also access the form via O' Connor's website at* <u>*bit.ly/HomesteadExemptionForm*</u>.

Types of residential homestead exemption include *general, over 65, disabled, disabled veteran and surviving spouse of a first responder.*

The amount of residential homestead exemption varies from county to county and tax entity to tax entity. The following chart shows the **mandatory exemption** throughout Texas:

MANDATORY RESIDENTIAL EXEMPTION IN TEXAS

	School	City	County	Special District
General	$25,000	-0-	$3,000 from farm-to-market/ flood control tax if levied	-0-
Over 65	$ 10,000 additional	-0-	-0-	-0-
Disabled	$ 10,000 additional	-0-	-0-	-0-

Note:—A person eligible for both disabled and over 65 exemption receives only one.

Chapter 5, Table 1

O'Connor Tax Reduction Experts 713.369.5958

To view and download the Homestead Exemption form, go to bit.ly/HomesteadExemptionForm.

As you can see, *mandatory exemptions* deal primarily with school taxes. There are additional *optional exemptions* which taxing entities may offer. **To determine which residential homestead exemptions are offered in your area, call the individual taxing entities for your homestead, i.e., the local school district, the city, the county, and the MUD (if there is one in your area).**

The following is a summary of the other property-tax exemptions which may be available for the Texas property owner:

Agriculture–Special agriculture valuation sharply reduces property taxes.

Timber–Special timber value sharply cuts property taxes.

Public property–Property owned by the state or a political subdivision of the state is exempt if used for public purposes.

Public property used to provide transitional housing for indigent persons–A taxing unit by ordinance or order may be exempt from ad valorem taxation if it is owned by the United States or an agency of the United States and used to provide transitional housing for the indigent under a program operated or directed by the United States Department of Housing and Urban Development.

Federal Exemptions–Property exempt from ad valorem taxation by federal law is exempt from taxation. Property owned by the United States government is generally not subject to Texas property taxes.

Tangible Personal Property Not Producing Income–All tangible personal property, other than manufactured homes, that a person owns and which is not held or used for the production of income is exempt from Texas property taxes.

Note–A person, as defined by the Texas Property Tax Code, includes both an individual and an entity such as a corporation or limited partnership.

Income-producing tangible property having a value of less than $500–A person (or business) is entitled to an exemption from taxation on the tangible personal property that person owns that is held or used for the production of income if the property has an aggregate taxable value of less than $500.

Mineral interests having a value of less than $500–A person is entitled to an exemption from taxation of the mineral interest that person owns, if the mineral interest the person owns has a value of less than $500.

Note–the primary reason for the last two exemptions, for property having a value of less than $500, is to reduce the burden on the appraisal district for assessing it and the tax entities for collecting the tax. The cost of assessing, billing, accounting, and collecting the taxes probably would exceed the amount of the taxes.

Farm Products–Farm products including livestock and poultry under the ownership of a person who is financially providing for the physical requirements of such livestock and poultry on January 1 of the tax year are exempt from taxation.

A plant nursery is a farm product for the purposes of this exemption if it is growing plants.

Implements of farming and ranching which are personal property are exempt from ad valorem taxation.

Cemeteries–Cemeteries are exempt from taxation if they are used exclusively for human burial and the property is not held for a profit.

Charitable Organizations–Property owned by a charitable organization is exempt from taxation if it is used exclusively to perform a religious, charitable, scientific, literary, or educational purpose. It is not exempt if used for profit.

Charitable organizations improving property for low-income housing–Real property or personal property owned by this type of organization is exempt from taxation if the entity is a charitable organization as defined in the Texas Property Tax Code; owns the property for the purpose of building or repairing housing on the property primarily with volunteer labor to sell without profit to low-income families or individuals; and engages exclusively in the building, repair, and sale of housing and related activities.

Community housing development organizations improving property for low-income and moderate-income housing–This type of organization is entitled to an exemption if it is organized as a community housing development organization; is a charitable organization as defined by the Texas Property Tax Code; owns the property for the purpose of building or repairing housing on the property to sell without profit to a low-income or moderate-income individual or family or to rent without profit to such an individual or family; and engages exclusively in the building, repair, and sale or rental of housing in related activities.

Youth, spiritual, mental, and physical development associations–Property owned by a youth development association is exempt from taxation if it is organized and operated primarily for the purpose of promoting the threefold spiritual, mental, and physical development of boys, girls, young men, or young women and is operated in a way that does not result in accrual of distributable profits. There are other technical qualifications.

Religious organizations–Property owned by a religious organization which is used primarily as a place of regular religious worship, and is reasonably necessary for engaging in religious worship, is exempt from Texas property taxes. There are various technical qualifications.

Schools–The building and tangible personal property reasonably necessary for the operation of a nonprofit school is exempt from taxation. There are additional technical requirements.

Disabled Veterans–A disabled veteran is entitled to a partial exemption depending upon the extent of his disability. The following table shows the exemptions for one property owned by the veteran.

EXEMPTION FOR DISABLED VETERANS

Disability Rating of:

At least	but not greater than	Amount
10%	30%	$5,000
30%	50%	$7,500
50%	70%	$10,000
70%		$12,000
10% and 65 or older		$12,000
Loss or loss of use of one or more limbs		$12,000
Total blindness in one or both eyes		$12,000
Paraplegia		$12,000

The spouse and children of a member of an armed force who dies while on active duty are entitled to an exemption of $ 5,000. **Veterans with a 100% disability that is service related receive a 100% exemption from property taxes for their homestead.**

Chapter 5, Table 2

There are miscellaneous exemptions for veteran's organizations, Federation of Women's Clubs, Nature Conservancy of Texas, Congress of Parents and Teachers, private enterprise demonstration associations, owners of bison and cattalo, theater schools, community service clubs, medical center developments, scientific research corporations, historic sites, and marine cargo containers used exclusively in international commerce. There are technical requirements for each exemption which are not discussed in detail since the level of interest for each is quite narrow. You can obtain more information on these exemptions by contacting a property tax consultant, obtaining a copy the Texas Property Tax Code from the state of Texas Comptroller's Office, or visiting the comptroller's website at www.cpa.state.tx.us/.

"Freeport" or Tangible Personal Property Exemption– "Freeport goods" are personal property that is transported outside of the state no later than 175 days after the date the person who owns it on January 1 acquired it or imported it into the state. There are detailed technical requirements for Freeport goods. In general, this is an exemption for personal property used in a manufacturing operation or held for distribution. Each taxing entity may elect whether to adopt the Freeport exemption. The Freeport exemption is used extensively by economic development groups to recruit new business. The Freeport exemption cannot be eliminated after it is elected by a tax entity.

Limitations of school tax on homesteads of the elderly– School taxes on the homestead of a person 65 or older may not increase beyond those established during the first year, provided there are no significant improvements to the property. There are detailed technical requirements regarding this exemption. In general, it extends to the surviving spouse if he or she is 55 or older and continues to use the property as his or her homestead. See chapter 6 on how not to pay school taxes after age 65.

Solar and wind-powered energy devices–Solar and wind-powered devices used primarily for the production and distribution of energy on a site are exempt from taxation.

Offshore drilling equipment not in use–Offshore drilling equipment being stored in a county bordering on the Gulf of Mexico or on a bay or other body of water immediately adjacent to the Gulf of Mexico which is not being stored for the sole purpose of repair or maintenance and is not being used to drill a well at the location at which it is being stored is exempt from property taxes.

Property exempted from city taxation by agreement–The owner of property subject to a Property Redevelopment and Tax Abatement Act agreement is entitled to exemption from taxation by an incorporated city or town or another taxing district (of all or part of the value of the property) as provided by the agreement.

Intracoastal Waterway dredge disposal site—Land being used as a disposal site for depositing and discharging materials dredged from the main channel of the Gulf Intracoastal Waterway is exempt from taxation. This exemption terminates when the site is no longer dedicated to that purpose.

Nonprofit water supply or Wastewater Service Corporation–Subject to technical requirements, a nonprofit organization dedicated to distributing water and providing wastewater service is exempt from taxation.

Pollution control equipment–Subject to detailed technical requirements, pollution control equipment can be exempt from property taxes.

While there are many different exemptions available for specific types of property in Texas, the most commonly used are those for residential homesteads and for disabled veterans. The other exemptions are narrowly tailored for specific types of property and of limited interest to most people.

Special Offer to purchasers of

"Cut Your Texas Property Taxes"

Get a FREE evaluation to determine if you are being
overtaxed with our Texas Fairness Checker

Go to www.CutMyTaxes.com

Chapter 6: How To Pay No Property Taxes After Age 65 In Texas

If you have to continue paying property taxes, do you own your home or just rent it from the government? Wouldn't it be great if there were a way to enjoy the golden years without the burden of paying property taxes? Well, there are options. Of course, there are also tradeoffs.

SCHOOL VERSUS CITY AND COUNTY TAXES

There is a clever, unknown trick to not pay school property taxes after you turn age 65 in Texas. Exemption from city and county taxes is possible but options vary from entity, to entity depending on the amount of exemption.

Really? I don't have to Pay School Taxes after 65?

The trick involves an obscure provision in the Tax Code that allows for "portability" of school taxes. Let's start with the basics.

CAP AT 65

School property taxes are frozen at age 65 unless you remodel or enlarge your house. However if you move at age 70 or 75 or 80, you would want the same relative benefit from the tax freeze. That is the function of the portability provision. For example, if your school property taxes were frozen at $300,000 and at age 75 you sell that house (and at the time the assessed value is $500,000). So the frozen tax value is 60% of market value. That same fraction will apply whether you buy a larger or smaller house.

BUT HOW DO I GET TO 0%?????????????????????

Simple. Purchase a property in a school district that has a high enough over-65 exemption. Each school district in Texas sets its own over-65 exemption, with a minimum of $10,000. Houston Independent School District has a $15,000 over-65 exemption but La Porte has a $60,000 over-65 exemption. There is plenty of single-family housing that can be purchased for $60,000.

NEXT STEP

About a year before you turn age 65, buy and move into a

home valued at less than the ISD exemption. For example, assume you move to the La Porte ISD and buy a house valued at $50,000. Your school property taxes would be $0. Let's assume you live in the La Porte ISD home for two years. Your taxes are still $0. Now assume you buy home value at $500,000. Your taxes would increase relative to the value of the houses. For example: $0 x ($500,000/$50,000) = $0

Zero times any number is zero. If you live in a home valued at less than the school district exemption, you do not have to pay school taxes the balance of your life.

The other taxes are typically city, county, and perhaps MUD. Unfortunately, you may still be required to pay MUD taxes. However, there are options to avoid paying city and county property taxes. For example, both the City of Houston and Harris County have an over-65 homestead exemption of $160,000.

WHAT IF I BUY A HOUSE IN HOUSTON VALUED AT LESS THAN $160,000?

Yes, to complete the process, find a house where the over-65 homestead exemption is more than the value of the house.

BUT I WANT A NICE HOUSE!

Great, just realize you will have to pay the property taxes or let them accrue at 8% (as of 2018). More information will be covered on accrual below.

Life involves choices. Most readers are unlikely to be willing to live in a house valued below the school district's over-65 exemption. Living in a house valued less than the over-65 school exemption is the "price" you pay to not pay school taxes after age 65. Some people will choose temporary discomfort for substantial long-term savings. At the age of 65, if you live in a $300,000 house with a $1.5% tax rate, the annual taxes are $4,500 and if you live to be 80 years old, the taxes for 15 years are $67,500.

One of the earliest points made in this book is that by selecting the value of your home, you are electing how much you will pay in property taxes. Property taxes are referred to "ad valorem;" based on value.

CITY AND COUNTY TAXES

As you select where to live after age 65, you should consider the level of homestead exemption. Over-65 homestead exemptions range from $10,000 to $160,000 in Harris County. Even if you do not elect to live in a house valued at less than the over-65 homestead exemption for city and county, you can still make a large impact. For example, in

Harris County a median priced home is $230,000. In this case, the homeowner would pay city and county property taxes based on only 30% of the value of the property.

PROPERTY TAX DEFERRAL AFTER AGE 65

When the first spouse turns age 65, it is possible to put property taxes on an accrual at 8%, due when the second spouse passes. Whether this make sense depends on your circumstances. If your retirement savings is more than ample to last your lifetime, 8% probably seems like a high interest rate compared to the other options.

If you are living on social security and have limited other resources, this is a great way to reduce your out-of-pocket expenses.

The ability to accrue taxes depends on whether you have a mortgage. If you have a mortgage on the house, you probably will not be able to accrue. However, you could consider a reverse mortgage on your house that might even provide you with a monthly payment if you are real estate rich and cash poor.

Consider a widow living in a $500,000 home with a limited social security payment. However, the home is owned free and clear. She could arrange for a reverse mortgage to provide a meaningful monthly payment for the balance of her life, whether she lives to be 70 or 100. (Note – I do not sell reverse mortgages.)

CONCLUSION

Most readers will probably not move to a quite modest home to avoid paying school taxes after age 65. But at least you know of the option. And you might know someone who should consider it. ou also learned about the large variations of over-65 exemptions for cities and counties. Finally, in many cases, you can stop paying property taxes after age 65 (and let them accrue) and now you know about the option to get a monthly check based on your free and clear home.

Chapter 7: Types Of Protests

Taking advantage of all available tax exemptions will lower your property taxes but does nothing to lower the *value* set on your property by the central appraisal district. **To lower the value, you must go through the appraisal protest process.**

A property owner can protest a variety of issues. **The most typical type of protest is a timely protest that the assessed value of a property is higher than market value.** Sections 41.41, 41.411, 41.412, 41.413, 41.42, 41.43 and 25.25 are the primary sections of the Texas Property Tax Code which designate when a property owner may protest. The following is the content of each of these sections along with brief explanation:

Sec: 41.41–RIGHT OF PROTEST

A property owner is entitled to protest before the appraisal review board the following actions:

determination of the appraised value of the owner's property or, in the case of appraised as provided by Subchapter C, D, E, or H, Chapter 23, determination of its appraised or market value;

Most protests are filed under 41.41a1. This section allows the property owner to protest the **assessed value**. In most cases, the property owner believes that the market value is less than the assessed value.

unequal appraisal of the owner's property;

A property owner's right to protest an unequal appraisal of the owner's property (Section 41.41a2) is what is commonly called a "uniform and equal" or an equity protest. Since a property owner should not be taxed more heavily than his neighbors, this section allows a property owner to protest if he believes his assessment is high compared to the assessment of similar properties.

 PRACTICE TIP–File your protest for both assessed value over market value and unequal appraisal even if you believe you will only receive a reduction on one and not the other. The appraisal district's evidence may support a reduction in the option you did not believe would support a reduction.

inclusion of the owner's property on the appraisal records;

Subsection 41.41a3 allows a property owner to protest the inclusion of property on the appraisal records which should not be included on the appraisal records since it is either not taxable or does not exist.

denial to the property owner in whole or in part of a partial exemption;

Subsection 41.41a4 addresses exemptions.

determination that the owner's land does not qualify for appraisal as provided by Subchapter C, D, E, or H, Chapter 23;

Subsection 41.41a5 addresses agricultural use and timber use exemptions (steeply reduced assessed values for taxation purpose).

identification of the taxing units in which the owner's property is taxable in the case of appraisal district's appraisal roll;

Subsection 41.41a6 addresses which tax entities are entitled to tax the property owner. Protests under this section are uncommon.

determination that the property owner is the owner of the property;

Subsection 41.41a7 addresses ownership of the property being assessed. Since property taxes of personally owned property are a personal obligation, it is prudent to protest if you are incorrectly listed as the owner of the property.

a determination that a change in use of land appraised under Subchapter C, D, E, or H, Chapter 23, has occurred; or

Subsection 41.41a8 addresses a change in an agricultural use or a timber use designation; these designations sharply reduce the taxes. Hence, the loss of these designations would dramatically increase property taxes. It may also cause a rollback of taxes. This means the owner has to pay five years back taxes based on the market value instead of the favorable agricultural or timber value. Based on a 3% tax rate and the same value for 5 years, the rollback taxes are 15% of the appraisal district's value.

Any other action of the chief appraiser, appraisal district, or appraisal review board that applies to and adversely affects the property owner.

Subsection 41.41a9 is an infrequently used catchall provision. O'Connor includes it in their property tax protests. We include the unlawful behavior of the appraisal districts and appraisal review boards.

Each year the chief appraiser for each appraisal district shall publicize in a manner reasonably designed to notify all residents of the district:

the provisions of this section; and

the method by which a property owner may protest an action before the appraisal review board.

Subsection 41.41b requires the chief appraiser to notify residents of the right to protest and how to file a protest. This information is printed in a local newspaper.

Sec, 41.411–PROTEST OF FAILURE TO GIVE NOTICE

A property owner is entitled to protest before the appraisal review board the failure of the chief appraiser or the appraisal review board to provide or deliver any notice to which the property owner is entitled.

Subsection 41.411a is used primarily to protest that a property owner has not received notice of a change in the assessed value as required by the Texas Property Tax Code. It can also be used to protest not having received any other notice such as a property tax hearing notice or a change in exemption status. The chief appraiser is required to notify the property owner if the assessed value increases by more than $1,000. The chief appraiser is not required to send a notice of assessed value if the value does not change, decreases, or increases by less than $1,000.00.

If failure to provide or deliver the notice is established, the appraisal review board shall determine a protest made by the property owner on any other grounds of protest authorized by this title relating to the property to which the notice applies.

Subsection 41.411b allows a property owner to have a protest hearing if he wasn't given notice by the chief appraiser or the appraisal review board.

A property owner who protests as provided by this section must comply with the payment requirements of Section 42.08 or he forfeits his right to a final determination of his protest.

Subsection 41.411c requires timely payment of property taxes by the property owner in order to prevail on a protest under Section 41.411.

For example, if a property owner does not receive notice that his assessed value is increasing from $100,000 to $500,000, does not file a timely protest, and does not pay the undisputed amount of property taxes timely, he loses his right to protest. Even though the appraisal district did not give the appropriate notice of an increase in value, the property owner may not protest (under 41.411a) since taxes were not paid timely. If the owner believed the value was $100,000, he could pay taxes on a value of $100,000 and continue the appeal. However, if the final value is higher, penalties and interest will be due on the amount in excess of $100,000.

Sec. 41.412–PERSON ACQUIRING PROPERTY AFTER JANUARY 1

A person who acquires property after January 1 and before the deadline for filing a notice of the protest may pursue a protest under this subchapter in the same manner as a property owner who owned the property on January 1.

Subsection 41.412a allows a property owner who acquires property after January 1 and before the protest deadline to protest the property value as if he had owned the property on January 1.

If during the pendency of a protest under this subchapter the ownership of the property subject to the protest changes, the new owner of the property on application to the appraisal review board may proceed with the protest in the same manner as the property owner who initiated the protest.

If property ownership changes during the time a protest is pending, the new owner may continue the protest as if he had filed the protest.

Practice Tip–It would probably be more productive for the former owner or a property tax agent to attend the hearing. Once the appraisal district learns of the sale, it will want a copy of the closing statement. Unless the property sold for less than the assessed value, providing the closing statement could increase the assessed value.

Sec. 41.413–PROTEST BY PERSON LEASING PERSONAL PROPERTY

A person leasing tangible personal property who is contractually obligated to reimburse the property owner for taxes imposed on the property is entitled to protest before the appraisal review board a determination of the appraised value of the property if the property owner does not file protest relating to the property.

A tenant leasing tangible personal property (also referred to as business personal property or BPP) who is responsible for paying property taxes or reimbursing the property owner for property taxes is entitled to protest if the property owner does not file a protest. Intangible personal property (computer programs, accounts receivable, etc.) is not taxable.

A person leasing real property who is contractually obligated to reimburse the property owner for taxes imposed on the property is entitled to protest before the appraisal review board a determination of the appraised value of the property if the property owner does not file a protest relating to the property. The protest provided by this subsection is limited to a single protest by either the property owner or the lessee.

A tenant leasing real property who is responsible for paying property taxes or reimbursing the property owner for property taxes is entitled to protest if the property owner does not file a protest.

Only one protest may be filed (either by the property owner or the lessee).

A person bringing a protest under this section is considered the owner of the property for purposes of the protest. The appraisal review board shall deliver a copy of any notice relating to the protest and of the order determining the protest to the owner of the property and the person bringing the protest.

This requires that notice is sent to the person filing the protest regardless of whether it is the property owner or the lessee.

The property owner shall timely send to the person leasing the property a copy of any notice of the property's reappraisal received by the property owner. Failure of the owner to send a copy of the notice to the person leasing the property does not affect the time within which the person leasing the property may protest the appraised value.

A person leasing property under a contract described by this section may request that the chief appraiser of the appraisal district in which the property is located send the notice described by Subsection (d) to the person. Except as provided by Subsection (f), the chief appraiser shall send the notice to the person leasing the property not later than the fifth day after the date the notice is sent to the property owner if the person demonstrates that the person is contractually obligated to reimburse the property owner for the taxes imposed on the property.

A chief appraiser who receives a request under Subsection (e) is not required to send the notice requested under that subsection if the appraisal district in which the property that is the subject of the notice is located posts the appraised value of the property on the district's Internet website not later than the fifth day after the date the notice is sent to the property owner.

A person leasing property under a contract described by this section may designate another person to act as the agent of the lessee for any purpose under this title. The lessee must make the designation in the manner provided by Section 1.111. An agent designated under this subsection has the same authority and is subject to the same limitations as an agent designated by a property owner under Section 1.111.

Section 41.413d requires the property owner to send the tenant notice of the change in assessed value which the property owner received. In other words, it is not the responsibility of the appraisal district to identify the tenant and send him notice of a change in assessed value.

Sec. 41.42–PROTEST OF SITUS

A protest against the inclusion of property on the appraisal records for an appraisal district on the ground that the property does not have taxable situs in that district shall be determined in favor of the protesting party if he establishes that the property is subject to appraisal by another district or that the property is not taxable in this state. The chief appraiser of a district in which the property owner prevails in a protest of situs shall notify the appraisal office of the district in which the property owner has established situs.

This section states that property owner need pay property taxes to only 1 county in the state of Texas or may protest if the property is not taxable in Texas. For example, suppose construction company uses heavy equipment in 15 counties during a tax year and its home office is in Harris County; it would not be appropriate for all 15 counties to assess and tax the property. This property is most often taxable in the location where it is stored when not being used–**in this example, in Harris County.**

Sec.41.43–PROTEST OF INEQUALITY OF APPRAISAL

In a protest authorized by Section 41.41(1) or (2), the appraisal district has the burden of establishing the value of the property by a preponderance of the evidence presented at the hearing. If the appraisal district fails to meet that standard, the protest shall be determined in favor of the property owner.

Section 41.43a gives the appraisal district the burden of proof supporting its determination of appraised value. This section was added by the 1997 legislature. Unfortunately, as of early 2001, many appraisal review boards appear to give more credence to the initial assessed value generated by the mass appraisal computer model which generates a predetermined value in violation of the Uniform Standards of Professional Appraisal Practice (USPAP) than to the evidence presented by the property owner.

Since our firm, O'Connor, handles over 100,000 tax protests in Texas annually, we have the best understanding of what is occurring in the appraisal review boards regarding unequal appraisal. Unfortunately, the reports from our consultants are uniformly bleak. Appraisal review boards, with very few exceptions, uniformly rule in favor of unlawful appraisal district evidence. The evidence is unlawful because appraisal districts use circular math to generate a predetermined result. Using the appraisal district's model, one could adjust an outhouse to a mansion fit for a king, and the adjusted value would match within $1.00. Think about it. Could you make "appropriate" adjustments to adjust an outhouse to a mansion and have the adjusted value match exactly? Of course, you can't. No one would expect the appraisal district to win 999 out of 1,000 hearings on unequal appraisal. But appraisal districts do win 99.9% of the time on unequal appraisal.

The logical questions are 1) Can we trust the appraisal review boards and 2) what changes would fix the problem?

A protest on the ground of unequal appraisal of property shall be determinate in favor of the protesting party unless the appraisal district establishes that the appraisal ratio of the property is not greater than the median level of appraisal of:

a reasonable and representative sample of other properties in the appraisal district;

a sample of properties in the appraisal district consisting of a reasonable number of other properties similarly situated to, or of the same general kind or character as, the property subject to the protest:

or

a reasonable number of comparable properties appropriately adjusted.

Subsection 41.43b allows protest based on inequality of assessment (uniform and equal). Substations "b1" and "b2" address using a ratio study to protest unequal appraisal. Subsection "b3" is a new section (added in 1997) which allows a protest based on using appropriately adjusted assessment comparables. The introduction to subsection "b" gives the appraisal district the burden of proof in an unequal appraisal hearing if the protest is filed by the property owner.

For purposes of this section, evidence includes the data, schedules, formulas, or other information used to establish the matter at issue.

Subsection 41.43c defines evidence for purpose of section 41.43.

Sec.25.25–CORRECTION OF APPRAISAL ROLL

Except as provided by Chapters 41 and 42 of this code and by this section, the appraisal roll may not be changed.

Assessed values and property tax records may not be changed arbitrarily.

The chief appraiser may change the appraisal roll at any time to correct a name or address, a determination of ownership, a description of the property, multiple appraisals of a property, or a clerical error or other inaccuracy as prescribed by board rule that does not increase the amount of tax liability. Before the 10th day after the end of each calendar quarter, the chief appraiser shall submit to the appraisal review board and to the board of directors of the appraisal district a written report of each change made under this subsection that decreases the tax liability of the owner of the property. The report must include:

 a description of each property

and

the name of the owner of that property.

The chief appraiser may change the appraisal roll at any time to correct errors if it does not increase the property owner's liability. If the appraisal district tells you, "there is nothing we can do," perhaps you can remind them of Section 25.25b of the Texas Tax Code.

The appraisal review board, on motion of the chief appraiser or of a property owner, may direct by written order changes in the appraisal roll for any of the five preceding years to correct:

clerical errors that a property owner's liability for a tax imposed in that tax year,

multiple appraisals of a property in that tax year,

or

the inclusion of property that does not exist in the form or at the location described in the appraisal roll.

This section allows for a reduction in property taxes going back four to five years for clerical errors in the tax roll, multiple appraisals in a tax year, or incorrect inclusion of the property in the appraisal roll. Most appraisal districts are reluctant to use this section expect in the case of significant errors. For example, if a 1,000-square-foot house is listed on the tax rolls as having 2,000 square feet, the appraisal district is likely to agree with a correction going back four to five years under this section. However, if a 1,000-square-foot house is listed as having 1,050 square feet, the appraisal district is unlikely to agree to a four-to-five-year adjustment in property taxes.

At any time prior to the date that the taxes become delinquent, a property owner or the chief appraiser may file a motion with the appraisal review board to change the appraisal roll to correct an error that resulted in an incorrect appraised value of the owner's property. However, the error may not be corrected unless it resulted in an appraised value that exceeds by more than one-third the correct appraised value. If the appraisal roll is changed under this subsection, the property owner must pay to each affected taxing unit a late-correction penalty equal to 10 percent of the amount of taxes as calculated on the basis of the corrected appraised value. Payment of the late-correction penalty is secured by the lien that attaches to the property under Section 32.01 and is subject to enforced collection under Chapter 33. The roll may not be changed under this subsection if: (1) the property was the subject of a protest brought by the property owner under Chapter 41, a hearing on the protest was conducted in which the property owner offered evidence or argument, and the appraisal review board made a determination of the protest on the merits; or (2) the appraised value of the property was established as a result of a written

agreement between the property owner or the owner's agent and the appraisal district.

Section 25.25d allows a property owner to file a protest for property not protested during the normal protest season if the assessed value is more than one-third greater than the correct assessed value. The property owner is required to pay a 10% late correction penalty. Even if the property owner does not prevail at the 25.25d hearing, it is often possible to obtain tax reduction through a judicial appeal.

If the chief appraiser and the property owner do not agree to the correction before the 15th day after the date the motion is filed, a party bringing a motion under Subsection (c) or (d) is entitled on request to a hearing on and a determination of the motion by the appraisal review board. A party bringing a motion under this section must describe the error or errors that the motion is seeking to correct. Not later than 15 days before the date of the hearing, the board shall deliver written notice of the date, time, and place of the hearing to the chief appraiser, the property owner, and the presiding officer of the governing body of each taxing unit in which the property is located. The chief appraiser, the property owner, and each taxing unit are entitled to present evidence and argument at the hearing and to receive written notice of the board's determination of the motion. A property owner who files the motion must comply with the payment requirements of Section 25.26 or forfeit the right to a final determination of the motion.

This section requires 15 days notice for a hearing under subsection "c" or "d" and timely payment of property taxes. The party filing a protest may request a hearing be scheduled. Some appraisal districts have previously declined or delayed scheduling 25.25c and d hearings. There is an exception for timely payment of taxes if the taxpayer is unable to pay the taxes.

The chief appraiser shall certify each change made as provided by this section to the assessor for each unit affected by the change within five days after the date the change is entered.

This section requires the chief appraiser to notify the assessor within 5 days after change is made.

Within 60 days after receiving notice of the appraisal review board's determination of a motion under this section or of a determination of the appraisal review board that the property owner has forfeited the right to a final determination of a motion under this section for failing to comply with the prepayment requirements of Section 25.26, the property owner or the chief appraiser may file suit to compel the board to order a change in the appraisal roll as required by this section. A taxing unit may not be made a party to a suit filed by a property owner or chief appraiser under this subsection.

This section allows the property owner or the chief appraiser to file a lawsuit to appeal the decision by the appraisal review board.

The appraisal review board, on the joint motion of the property owner and the chief appraiser filed at any time prior to the date the taxes become delinquent, shall by written order correct an error that resulted in an incorrect appraised value for owner's property.

This section requires the appraisal review board to correct an error in an appraised (assessed) value at any time prior to the delinquency date (typically February 1 of the subsequent year) if it has been jointly filed by the property owner and the chief appraiser.

You can see that there are many options available for filing a protest. However, **most protests are filed because the property owner believes the property is assessed for more than market value or is unequally assessed compared to nearby properties.** We will focus mostly on these types of protests in this book.

Chapter 8: How To File A Protest

This chapter addresses the timing and mechanics of filing a property tax protest in Texas. Remember, **filing a protest is a simple process: you must file it timely, describe the property being protested, list the property owner, and state the reason (s) for the protest**.

First and foremost, it is crucial to keep in mind the following dates which are important to most Texas Property taxpayers:

January 1–Effective date for valuation in determining market value.

May 15–the protest deadline had been May 31 for about forty years. In 2018, the deadline changed to May 15 to file a notice of protest in most cases. Technically, the deadline to file a protest is the latter of May 15 or 30 days after notice of assessed value is mailed, if the assessed value was increased by more than $1,000. This is the deadline for a normal protest.

May/June/July/August/September–is the time period when most protest hearings are conducted.

August/September/October–the tax entities review the received tax roll and determine the tax rate for the following year.

December–Property taxes are due.

January 31–is the last day to pay property taxes for the previous year without a penalty.

Note– Although property taxes are due on receipt of the bill under Section 31.02, there is no penalty if they are paid on or before January 31 for the previous year.

January 31 is also the last day to file a 25.25h or 25.25d protest for the previous year.

These protest deadlines are extended to the following business day if the date falls on a weekend or recognized holiday.

Texas Property Tax Code, Section 41.44, describes how to file a protest. The following is the content of Section 41.44:

Sec. 41.44–NOTICE OF PROTEST

Except as provided by Subsections (b), (b-1), (c), (c-1), and (c-2), to be entitled to a hearing and determination of a protest, the property owner initiating the protest must file a written notice of the protest with the appraisal review board having authority to hear the matter protested before May 16 or not later the 30th day after the date that notice was delivered to the property owner as provided by Section 25.19, whichever is later:

This is the provision which affects most taxpayers. If there is any doubt, file a protest on or before May 15 of each year.

in the case of a protest of a change in the appraisal records ordered as provided by Subchapter A of this chapter or by Chapter 25, not later than the 30th day after the date notice of the change is delivered to the property owner,

or

in the case of a determination that a change in the use of land appraised under Subchapter C, D or E, Chapter 23, has occurred, not later than the 30th day after the date the notice of the determination is delivered to the property owner.

A property owner who files a notice of protest after the deadline prescribed by Subsection (a) of this section but before the appraisal review board approves the appraisal records is entitled to a hearing and determination of the protest if he shows good cause as determined by the board for failure to file the notice on time.

PRACTICE TIP–Forgetting the deadline, being busy, or having more important tasks is not considered "good cause" by the appraisal district. If you are not sure whether or not you want to protest, file a protest by May 31 and evaluate evidence for the hearing late. You can always withdraw the protest before the hearing if you decide it is not warranted.

A property owner who files notice of a protest authorized by Section 41.411 is entitled to a hearing and determination of the protest if he files the notice prior to the date the taxes on the property to which the notice applies becomes delinquent. An owner of land who files a notice of protest under Subsection (a) (3) is entitled to a hearing and determination of the protest without regard to whether the appraisal records are approved.

This convoluted language means that, if you are protesting that the appraisal district did not provide a required notice, you are required to file the protest by January 31 of the following year or before taxes become delinquent, whichever is later.

A notice of protest is sufficient if it identifies the protesting property owner, including a person claiming an ownership interest in the property even if that person is not listed on the appraisal records as an owner of the property, identifies the property that is the subject of the protest, and indicates apparent dissatisfaction with some determination of the appraisal office. The notice need not be on an official form, but the comptroller shall prescribe a form that provides for more detail about the nature of the protest. The form must permit a property owner to include each property in the appraisal district that is the subject of a protest. The comptroller, each appraisal office, and each appraisal review board shall make the forms readily available and deliver one to a property owner on request.

The Texas Property Tax Code does not require the protest to be on an official form as long as it identifies the protesting property owner, identifies the property, and indicates dissatisfaction with some determination of the appraisal office (i.e., the property is overvalued or not uniformly and equally assessed).

The following is a sample letter of protest which could be used instead of a protest form:

O'Connor Tax Reduction Experts 713.369.5958

Mr. Chief Appraiser

Any Place Central Appraisal District

123 Jones Street

Your City, Texas, 77018

Re: Property at 123 West Phoenix Avenue

Dear Mr. Chief Appraiser:

Please consider this notice under Section 41.44 of a property tax protest of the above-referenced property since it is assessed for more than market value and is not assessed in a uniform and equal manner, and any other action of the chief appraiser, appraisal district, or appraisal review board that applies to and adversely affects the property owner.

Sincerely,

Ima Patriot

Property Owner

The letter protesting the property taxes does not need to be detailed or long as the technical requirements to file a protest are minimal. The letter may be typed or handwritten. As will be addressed in the next section, the letter can also request that the central appraisal district provide evidence they may present at the appraisal review board.

Changes made in 1997 to the Texas Property Tax Code allow a person protesting taxes to request an evening or weekend hearing. Each appraisal district is required to accommodate property owners who request a hearing during these times. There has not been a large demand for the evening and weekend hearings.

OPTIONS WHEN PROTESTING; OBTAIN THE APPRAISAL DISTRICT'S EVIDENCE FOR THE HEARING

The property owner can request that the appraisal district provide a copy of the evidence they will present at the hearing. They can't charge more than $15 for a house and $25 for a commercial property. In most cases, the fees are $0.10 per page and total less than $1.00.

 PRACTICE TIP–If an appraisal district tries to charge you $15 for 2 or 3 sheets of paper, tell them, "no thanks." Use your phone or a scanner to obtain images that can be printed. The appraisal district is required to inform the property owner that the owner or his agent may inspect and obtain a copy of the data, schedules, formulas, and all other information the chief appraiser plans to introduce at the hearing to establish any matter at issue.

This requires the CAD to present all information that will be used at the hearing so that the property owner may study it. One of the key benefits of requesting the appraisal districts evidence is that it often contains information helpful to the property owner. O'Connor has been a pioneer in getting appraisal districts to comply with this law.

The former requires the appraisal district to provide evidence to the property owner if they request it and the latter prohibits the appraisal district from presenting evidence if they did not make it available to the property owner two weeks prior to the hearing.

The hearing evidence package often includes: 1) the detailed summary of the appraisal district's information on your property, 2) comparable sales for houses, 3) comparable sales for land and 4) an unequal appraisal analysis.

While many appraisal districts provide hearing evidence electronically, most appraisal districts appear to produce them manually. Also, the manually produced ones sometimes only have cherry-picked sales which support the appraisal districts value.

Another advantage is that the property owner will not be surprised by unexpected information during the hearing. Imagine you have just finished a detailed, color-coded presentation on why the value of your home should be no higher than $275,000. Right after you finish, the appraiser pulls out a listing brochure for your home which is currently on the market. The asking price is $350,000. No matter what you say, you have most likely lost credibility with the appraisal review board panel for that account and lost the hearing. Surprise information presented by the appraisal districts is almost never good news.

To request the appraisal district's hearing evidence, ask the appraisal district to provide it when you file your protest. There may be a nominal fee for the appraisal district to provide this information. Many appraisal districts do not charge any fees to provide the information to an individual taxpayer.

O'Connor Tax Reduction Experts 713.369.5958

WHAT NOT TO INCLUDE WHEN PROTESTING

In most circumstances, it is not helpful to tell the appraisal district your opinion of the value of your property when protesting.

Providing an opinion of value when protesting only sets a lower limit on the range of settlement during the protest hearing. It appears to become part of the permanent record at some appraisal districts, which can hamper tax reduction efforts for years into the future. Even if you uncover evidence supporting a lower value after the protest is filed but before the hearing, the appraiser hearing your protest will be unlikely to agree to value less than your opinion of value in the initial protest.

In many cases, it does not help to provide information that you will be presenting at the hearing.

Most appraisal districts do not have time to review documentation provided with a notice of protest. Processing protests filed near the deadline, which is when most of them are filed, is a peak-load challenge at the appraisal district. It is also a bottleneck since the appraisal review board cannot schedule a protest hearing until the notice of protest is processed and recorded. The clerical staff processing the notices of protests is not interested in information on the merits of the tax protest. They are probably measured by how many records they process and reviewing evidence would only slow their process.

Furthermore, the information you provide with the notice of protest could harm your cause by setting a higher floor on settlement negotiations. If you discover other information which supports an even lower value before the hearing, documentation provided with the protest letter could negatively affect your settlement negotiations.

One exception which merits consideration is sending a closing statement with your protest. If you recently purchased the property and it is assessed for more than the purchase price, many appraisal districts will reduce the assessed value to the purchase price upon receipt of this information. Some appraisal districts may even make the change without a hearing. Also, you can protest for a lower value based on unequal appraisal.

The following link contains a protest form promulgated by the state of Texas. Comments on completing this form are contained in the following link: bit.ly/Form2Protest.

Harris County Appraisal District
Information & Assistance Division
P.O. Box 922004
Houston TX 77292-2004
FORM 41.44 (8/16)

PROPERTY APPRAISAL NOTICE OF PROTEST

Save a Stamp!
File Online at www.hcad.org/iFile

If you want the appraisal review board (ARB) to hear and decide your case, you must file a written notice of protest with the ARB for the appraisal district that took the action you want to protest.

GENERAL INSTRUCTIONS: Pursuant to Tax Code Section 41.41, a property owner has the right to protest certain actions taken by the appraisal district. This form is for use by a property owner or designated agent who would like to have the ARB hear and decide a protest. If you are leasing the property, you are subject to the limitations set forth in Tax Code Section 41.413.

FILING DEADLINES: The usual deadline for filing your notice is midnight, May 31. A different deadline may apply in certain cases. For more information, see Page 2.

HCAD Account Number: Tax Year:

Step 1: Owner's or Lessee's Name and Address

Owner's or Lessee's First Name and Initial   Last Name

Owner's or Lessee's Current Mailing Address (number and street)

City, State, ZIP Code

Phone (area code and number)

This space is reserved for HCAD use only

NEWPT611

Step 2: Describe Property Under Protest

Give Street Address and City if Different from Step 1, or Legal Description if No Street Address

Mobile Homes (give make, model, and identification number)

Step 3: Check Reason(s) for Your Protest

Failure to check a box may result in your inability to protest an issue. If you check "value is over market value," you are indicating that the market value is excessive and your property would not sell for the amount determined by the appraisal district. If you check "value is unequal as compared to other properties," you are indicating that your property is not appraised at the same level as a representative sample of comparable properties, appropriately adjusted for condition, size, location, and other factors. Your property may be appraised at its market value, but be unequally appraised. An appraisal review board may adjust your value to equalize it with other comparable properties. Please check all boxes that apply in order to preserve your rights so that the appraisal review board may consider your protest according to law.

☐ Value is over market value.

☐ Value is unequal compared with other properties.

☐ Property should not be taxed in _____ (name of taxing unit)

☐ Failure to send required notice _____ (form)

☐ Exemption denied, modified, or cancelled.

☐ Property should not be taxed in this appraisal district.

☐ Change in use of land appraised as ag-use, open-space, or timber land.

☐ Ag-use, open-space, timber, or other special valuation denied, modified, cancelled.

☐ Owner's name incorrect.

☐ Property description incorrect.
  ☐ Improvement (structures, etc.)
  ☐ Land (attach copy of deed.)

☐ Other_____

Step 4: Give Facts That May Help Resolve Your Case

Continue on additional pages as needed

What do you think your property's value is? (Optional) $

Step 5: Check to Receive ARB Hearing Procedures

I want the ARB to send me a copy of its hearing procedures.   ☐ Yes   ☐ No *
*If your protest goes to a hearing, you will automatically receive a copy of the ARB's hearing procedures.

Step 6: Signature

☐ Signature of Owner   ☐ Signature of Lessee   ☐ Agent   Agent Code # _____

Print Name _____

Sign Here _____   Date _____

ADDITIONAL INFORMATION ON BACK

To view and download the Texas protest form, go to bit.ly/Form2Protest.

The form allows space to check the types of protest and an opinion of value. It is prudent to check as many types of protest that may possibly become relevant by the time of the

108

hearing. If you file a protest by sending a letter rather than the form, be certain to note all types of protest which you may want to address at the hearing. You may list them in the letter. *Most appraisal districts will not consider a type of protest unless it is included in the protest form/letter.* **Do not include an opinion of value on the form or in a letter.**

This often becomes an issue with protests regarding unequal appraisal. Many property owners are not aware that they have to select separate "check boxes" for 1) market value and 2) unequal appraisal. Further compounding the problem is that many property owners do not have a solid technical understanding of unequal appraisal. However, they have a visceral, primal belief that IT IS NOT FAIR THAT THEY ARE ASSESSED FOR MORE THAN NEIGHBORS WHO HAVE NICER HOUSES.

At the hearing, the appraisal district appraiser will be quick to shut down a presentation on unequal appraisal if the taxpayer did not "check the PO Box" for unequal appraisal on the protest form. Of course, this makes property owners furious. They were already frustrated about high property taxes. But they stepped up to attempt to get a fair tax assessment, only to be told by a bureaucrat that their appeal will not be considered since they did not complete the paperwork correctly.

As previously discussed, it is recommended that you do NOT list an opinion of value or send information or evidence (other than a closing statement if it helps your case) when filling a protest.

Filing a protest is a simple process. The critical elements are to file it timely, describe the property being protested, and list the property owner and reason(s) for dissatisfaction. At a minimum, include value over market and unequal appraisal as the basis for protesting.

PRACTICE TIP – The most important rule in minimizing your Texas property taxes is to protest to the highest level of appeal that is financially feasible every year. Remember, every single year.

Special Offer to purchasers of:

"Cut Your Texas Property Taxes"

Get a FREE evaluation to determine if you are being overtaxed with our Texas Fairness Checker

Go to www.CutMyTaxes.com

Chapter 9: Steps In The Texas Property Tax Appeal Process

The complete property tax appeal process consists of three steps:

Informal hearing

Appraisal review board (ARB) hearing

Judicial appeal (litigation), binding arbitration or State Office of Administrative Hearings (SOAH)

To provide perspective on the number of properties and appeals in Texas, consider the following data, compiled by the Texas Comptroller for the tax year 2016:

Total number of tax parcels in Texas	19,207,001	
Total number of protests	1,579,386	8%
Informal settlements	923,246	
Appraisal review board hearings/formal	338,630	

Judicial appeals (lawsuit in district court)	10,716	0.06% of all tax parcels
Binding arbitration filings	11,102	0.06% of all tax parcels
State Office of Administrative appeals	59	

The small number of appeals is amazing when considering the large number of overvalued properties. About 40% of all properties are valued in excess of the market, or about 8 million properties. In addition, about 10% to 20% of all properties are valued in excess of 110%, based on analysis and ratio studies performed by O'Connor over the last twenty years. The total number of properties valued in excess of 110% is 1.9 million to 3.8 million; however, the number of appeals is only 1.36 million.

Incredibly, only 1 in 10,000 accounts generated a binding arbitration appeal in 2015 and only 5 in 10,000 generated a judicial appeal. Only about 21,828 (10,716 judicial appeals plus 11,112 binding arbitrations) out of 19,207,001 tax parcels generated an appeal at the third level.

Since about 8 million properties are overvalued, it would seem there would be more appeals. There are likely several factors and beliefs that diminish enthusiasm for tax protests and they are: 1) time – everyone is busy, 2) the property owner is removed from writing the check to the tax entities since it is done by the mortgage servicer, 3) belief in the myth you can't beat city hall (69% of tax protests at the informal and formal levels were successful), 4) concern that the value could be increased (very unlikely), 5) concern that the appraisal district will coerce you into revealing improvements done at the house and 6) "I did not know I could protest."

There are potentially three steps to the appeals process: 1) informal hearing, 2) appraisal review board, and 3) judicial appeal, binding arbitration or Texas State Office of Administrative Hearings (SOAH). The protest process may be resolved at either of the first two steps. For example, a protest resolved satisfactorily at the informal hearing does not continue to the appraisal review board (ARB) hearing stage. In fact, a property value which is agreed to at the informal hearing *cannot* be further protested at ARB or through litigation.

However, if a property tax protest is continued through the ARB stage, the owner may file a judicial appeal or binding arbitration, but it is not required. The property owner may stop the property tax process at any one of the three stages if he is satisfied with the result. In fact, the property owner can file a protest and not attend the hearing.

 PRACTICE TIP–The author strongly encourages property owners to file a protest for each property each year and obtain the

appraisal district's evidence prior to the hearing. Simply send a notice of protest and include a request for the appraisal district's hearing evidence (see Texas Tax Code section 41.461).

After you receive and review the appraisal district's evidence, along with any evidence you obtain on your own, you will be prepared to make a decision on whether or not to attempt the informal hearing. Since 69% of informal hearings resulted in a reduction in taxes, attending the informal hearing typically makes sense.

However, if it does not make sense for you **to attend the hearing, you still have accomplished the following:**

➢ Reviewed appraisal district's detailed information on your property to check for errors.

➢ Obtained the appraisal district's valuation methodology for your property (could be cost, sales or income).

➢ Had a chance to evaluate whether your property value is fair based on market value.

➢ Had an opportunity to do your own evaluation of whether your property is unequally appraised.

> Obtained valuable market data for your property that could be helpful in making asset management decisions.

Gives you the peace of mind that your property taxes are reasonable.

Filing a property tax protest annually and reviewing the hearing evidence obtained from the appraisal district is an excellent way to inexpensively gather information about the value of your property. More importantly, you have an opportunity to evaluate the tax value with regard to both market value and unequal appraisal to see if there is room to reduce the value.

INFORMAL HEARING NOT STATUTORY

The informal hearing process that resolves about two-thirds of tax protests is not statutory. In other words, neither the taxpayer nor the appraisal district has a "right" to an informal hearing and neither can be compelled to participate in the informal hearing.

CULTURE VARIES BY APPRAISAL DISTRICT

The culture and personality of each appraisal district are revealed through how they manage their appraisers and how they treat the public when conducting informal hearings. For example, in one appraisal district in North Texas, tax consultants routinely bring the appraisal district staff bagels, donuts, large containers of Starbucks coffee and other goodies. However, in at least one appraisal district in the Houston area, the author believes bringing such goodies to the staff could result in criminal charges of attempted bribery.

O'Connor serves 110,000 clients and conducts about 160,000 property tax protests in about 140 counties, mostly in Texas, each year. We see a wide range of policies at the informal hearings. And the policies for informal hearings can even vary by property type within a county. For example, Fort Bend CAD settles most commercial informally but a smaller portion of the residential is settled informally. Dallas CAD settles only a limited portion of the residential informally but makes a good effort to settle the commercial informally. Tarrant CAD likes to settle commercial and residential informally. Brazoria CAD makes a good faith effort to settle both residential and commercial informally. And so it goes; there is one state Tax Code but over 250 county appraisal districts each interpreting it in their own way and reacting differently to political pressures.

The term "informal hearing" aptly describes the first step in the protest process. Some counties require the informal hearing to be conducted before the time of the appraisal review board hearing. Some appraisal districts will only schedule a formal hearing so in order to have an informal hearing you will need to go to the appraisal district before the date of your formal hearing. For example, in Dallas County, if you show up at the scheduled protest time, you will be directed to the appraisal review board hearing without an opportunity to have an informal hearing. Therefore, you need to inquire as to the timing of the informal hearing process in your county (see the list of appraisal districts in the addendum).

Other counties, such as Harris County, schedule a time for the informal hearing. From a practical perspective, this is often done to reduce the number of hearings the appraisal review board is required to perform. ARB hearings are more expensive to perform than informal hearings since they require more personnel.

APPRAISAL DISTRICT PERSPECTIVE ON INFORMAL HEARINGS

Rule Number 1–The appraisal district's staff will avoid doing anything that might get them in trouble or fired. So let's consider the competing objectives of the staff appraiser at an appraisal district doing informal hearings.

Rule Number 2–Most appraisal district staff does not care if you pay taxes of $1,000 or $10,000,000, provided it is legal and their value judgments will withstand scrutiny.

Rule Number 3–Most appraisal district appraisers will make small adjustments regularly to get appeals settled. Even without evidence, they would attempt to find a way to settle a property valued at $200,000 for $180,000 or $190,000. It is simpler to settle than to continue the appeal.

Rule Number 4–Making large adjustments can be difficult to impossible. Harris County Appraisal district staff will almost never make an adjustment over $100,000, by policy, for single-family property owners. Often they decline informal hearings for homes over $1,000,000 and just send them straight to the appraisal review board since the informal resolution rate is low.

It can also be difficult at some appraisal districts to get large changes approved, even if they appear warranted. While it would be ideal to resolve these issues informally, the appraiser has little incentive to approve a large reduction. Instead, they prefer to submit the protest to their superiors for approval, unless they are certain the change is warranted.

 PRACTICE TIP–The guiding light for many appraisal district staff is "will my decision concern my superiors," "will my decision be second-guessed," and "could my decision get me fired?"

Rule Number 5–Reread Dale Carnegie's *How to Win Friends and Influence People,* and use those techniques in a positive manner to effect settlement. Consider a twenty-minute hearing and let's assume the topic of discussion is tracked by time. In the **first hearing**, the valuation of the property was discussed by the property owner for eighteen minutes and the appraiser responded on valuation issues for the final two minutes.

In the **second hearing**, the property owner noticed the distinctive watch that the appraiser was wearing. The appraiser spent most of the next seventeen minutes discussing his watch, plans to go fishing and his recent vacation. The property owner responded with information on his travels for two minutes. THEN, **they spent one minute discussing the value of the property** and what change was reasonable.

 PRACTICE TIP–Which of these interactions do you believe would generate the best results? The author's personal experience is that the more time spent discussing topics other than the property and valuation the better the results are for the property owner.

In the ideal case, the property owner provides the appraiser with his files and then they visit on topics of mutual interest while the appraiser determines what values are comfortable to him; see Rules Number 1, 2 and 3.

DOES THE APPRAISER HAVE EGO INVESTED IN THE VALUE?

The appraiser who performs the informal hearing may or may not have set the assessed value for your property. In smaller counties, the appraiser who sets the value also conducts the informal hearing. In larger counties, such as Harris and Dallas counties, it is not practical for the person who set the assessed value for a particular property to perform the informal hearing, so the person performing the informal hearing typically has not set the assessed value for the property. However, if the person you are meeting did set the values, beware. Appraisers sometimes take property tax protests as a personal attack. This is unfortunate when it happens. Fortunately, most appraisers realize that there is a range of value for appraisal. Further, during the tax appeal season, it is necessary to resolve a number of the accounts.

ARBITRARY ELEMENTS RELATED TO THE INFORMAL HEARING APPRAISER

Portions of the property tax protest process are arbitrary. Arbitrary elements include the attitude of the appraiser, knowledge of the appraiser, sales in the appraisal district evidence package, and the culture of the appraisal district. One such arbitrary element is the skill and experience of the appraiser performing the informal hearing; he or she may have very limited training and experience or may have performed hearings for 20 years.

 PRACTICE TIP–Do not assume that the appraiser holding your hearing is an expert. Do try to develop a good relationship with them. Ask open-ended questions to give the appraiser a chance to speak.

The informal hearing allows the property owner an opportunity to present evidence explaining why he or she believes the property is overvalued or why it is not assessed on a uniform and equal basis. If the protest is for another purpose, such as an exemption, pertinent evidence may also be presented. The informal appraiser will consider the evidence presented by the property owner and typically counter with information he has available regarding market value for the subject property. In most large counties, staff appraisers can access market data and information on the subject electronically by computer. Typically, they use geographic information system (GIS) and detailed aerial maps in their presentation.

UNEQUAL APPRAISAL

Most appraisal districts are still reluctant to consider appeals based on the uniform and equal concept. They often report the uniform and equal presentation provided by the owner is not in an acceptable format. This claim is ironic since the unequal appraisal evidence presented by most appraisal districts generates a predetermined value. In some cases, it is a predetermined value disguised not to look like a predetermined value.

PRACTICE TIP–Consider an emotional appeal that the property value is not fair. What can you do?

In case this is not clear, I will use plain language. At the time of this writing (March 2018), in most appraisal districts in Texas, the staff is presenting information that is misleading and violates the Texas tax code. First, the unequal appraisal analysis appears to be a sophisticated analysis validating that the value set by the appraisal district either: 1) matches comps exactly or 2) matches the comps to within 1% or 2%. The problem is the results are circular math designed to ALWAYS support the appraisal district's value. ALWAYS AND EVERY TIME. Folks, this is misleading since typical taxpayers do not know they use circular math which ALWAYS supports the appraisal district's value. The violation of the law is the licensing by the Texas Department of Licensing and Regulation's appraisal district staff, licensed as "Property Tax Professionals." Property tax professionals must not be misleading and must follow the Uniform Standards of Professional Appraisal Practice (USPAP). The predetermined value generated by the appraisal district violates USPAP.

Based on the experience of the author and reports from other professional tax consultants, the unfortunate truth is that most appraisal districts and appraisal review boards still ignore the law with regard to unequal appraisal. Appraisal districts generally will not consider unequal appraisal at informal hearings and the appraisal review boards rule with the appraisal district over 99% of the time on unequal appraisal, even when the appraisal district's evidence generates a predetermined value. It is so bad that the appraisal review board will rule in favor of the appraisal district even when they have no evidence and the property owner has evidence!

Some appraisal districts are taking a difficult position. Appraisal districts that choose not to settle informally, and to also oppose an acceptable value at the appraisal review board, are basically inviting applications for binding arbitration and judicial appeals. Yet these same appraisal districts that make it most difficult to settle tax protests informally, express surprise when there is a volume of binding arbitration filings and judicial appeals.

This breakdown in the hearing process led O'Connor to increase binding arbitrations and to address unequal appraisal. In 2015, there were 2,522 binding arbitration cases filed in Texas. In 2016, O'Connor filed over 8,000 binding arbitration cases. O'Connor filed a similar number of binding arbitration cases in 2017.

The real solution is either for the appraisal review boards to police themselves and start delivering honest judgments on unequal appraisal or for the legislature to craft a solution.

LENGTH OF INFORMAL HEARINGS

An informal hearing typically lasts only 10 to 20 minutes. You may be required to wait up to several hours before the hearing process begins, but most hearings begin within 15 to 30 minutes of the scheduled time. The informal hearing can be a brief and effective mechanism to achieve a modest change in the assessed value of your property. The appraiser performing the informal hearing for the appraisal district often has limited latitude and cannot make significant changes without obtaining approval. If you are asking for a large change (perhaps over 10 percent of the assessed value), be prepared with incontrovertible data supporting your position.

You should protest the assessed value of your property annually. In many cases, it still makes sense to appeal even if the appraisal district did not revalue. The author strongly believes that appealing property taxes annually is the best process to minimize property taxes in Texas. In addition, it is necessary to appeal property taxes to the highest financially feasible level each year. *In some cases that is the informal hearing due to a good informal settlement. In many cases, for properties that have an ARB hearing, it does make sense to pursue either binding arbitration or a judicial appeal. In other cases, it is not practical, due to the value of the property or quality of the evidence. Remember, if you settle at the informal hearing, you have completed the property protest process for the year.* However, you may protest the value in subsequent years whether or not the assessed value increases.

126

APPRAISAL REVIEW BOARD HEARINGS

If a property owner is not satisfied with the assessed value offered by the staff appraiser at the informal hearing, he may continue the appeal to the appraisal review board (ARB). An offer made to settle the protest at the informal hearing is not guaranteed at the ARB hearing, which may conclude with a value higher than or lower than the assessed value offered at the informal hearing. The ARB hearing typically occurs the same day as the informal hearing. However, you may be required to wait an hour or two after the informal hearing before the start of the appraisal review board hearing. Some appraisal districts will only schedule a formal hearing so in order to have an informal hearing you will need to go to the appraisal district before the date of your formal hearing. Some appraisal districts schedule a date for an informal hearing and a second date for the formal hearing if needed. Most ARB hearings start within 30 minutes after the informal hearing. It also varies from appraisal district to appraisal district. To better manage expectations for the volume of staff needed for appraisal review board hearings, Harris County Appraisal District (HCAD) elected to hold informal hearings

and formal hearings (if necessary) on another day several weeks in the future.

The appraisal review board hearing is typically conducted by a three-member appraisal review board panel. It also includes an appraiser from the central appraisal district. In limited cases, there is a clerk or recording officer from the appraisal district, and finally the property owner or his agent. However, some appraisal district panels include up to seven or more appraisal review board members. However, for reasons related to cost, most appraisal review board panels have the minimum of three members.

The three members who form the ARB panel typically come from a larger appraisal review board, which is technically independent of the central appraisal district. In most counties, members of the panel are rotated to minimize their relationship to each other. The level of experience of the ARB members varies dramatically. Some have essentially no real estate experience while others are Realtors, commercial brokers, or developers.

As a practical matter, most ARB members have limited real estate experience and training. However, they do **undergo a one-day training process** mandated by state law before they can perform ARB hearings.

 PRACTICE TIP–Think about the level of responsibility and the level of training for ARB members. In one year, an ARB member could make decisions on 4,000 property tax appeals for property valued at $920 million ($200.000 per property) and total property taxes of $24,840,000. However they receive only one week of training which includes the Texas tax code, real estate valuation for land, single-family property, commercial property, hearing procedures, ARB rules, etc. The cost of one week of education is perhaps $500 to $1,000. It is impossible to do the necessary training in a week.

Both the ARB members and the property owner or his agent take an oath at the beginning of the hearing. The oath for the ARB members indicates that they swear that they have not discussed the property with each other or with members of the central appraisal district staff before the hearing. The property owner/agent's oath requires that they present information which they believe is accurate.

The steps in the ARB hearing include the following:

(1) Oaths

(2) Description of the property by CAD appraiser

(3) Presentation of evidence by the property owner

(4) Questions from ARB members

(5) Cross-examination of the property owner by the appraiser

(6) Presentation of evidence by CAD appraiser

(7) Questions from ARB members

(8) Cross-examination of the appraiser by the property owner

(9) Rebuttal by the property owner

(10) The decision by the ARB members

After a brief description of the property, the owner or his agent presents evidence regarding the owner's opinion of value. The property owner may also present evidence as to why he thinks the property is not assessed in a uniform and equal manner. Be forewarned that some appraisal districts are not inclined to consider evidence regarding a uniform and equal protest. However, you should present such evidence if you are considering a judicial appeal following the ARB hearing. The ARB members are given a chance to ask the owner or his agent questions. The CAD appraiser is then allowed to present evidence regarding his opinion of the value of the subject property.

For most properties, the ARB hearing lasts 15 to 20 minutes. There is an exception for large properties and complex situations. However, *in most cases, you will not be allowed to present evidence for more than 5 to 10 minutes regarding your property.*

PRACTICE TIP–If you have an unusual property, or complex issues to address in an appraisal review board hearing, advise the appraisal review board panel chairman at the beginning of the hearing. Be polite and professional. Acknowledge you understand the need to limit the time to present evidence. Give an overview of the types of issues involved and request their indulgence. Assure them you will present the information as quickly as possible. Consider asking them to let you know if you are overdoing an issue, if they already understand it.

After the property owner or his agent presents their evidence, the appraiser for the central appraisal district presents evidence or discusses why he believes some or all of the evidence presented by the property owner is not relevant. The members of the ARB often ask the property owner or staff appraiser questions regarding information they presented or their opinion of value. The ARB members then make a decision regarding the value.

The decision is presented to the property owner or agent at the hearing. The decision is subject to ratification by the full ARB (up to about 200 members in large counties) although it is highly unusual for the full panel not to ratify the decision of a three-member ARB panel. The official notice of the ARB hearing is typically mailed two to four weeks after the hearing. It is sent by certified mail to document the date of receipt. Some appraisal districts are now sending it electronically if agreeable to the owner or his/her agent.

Either the property owner or the chief appraiser who represents the appraisal district can appeal the result of the ARB hearing. (Tax entities cannot appeal.) In practice, a chief appraiser seldom files a judicial appeal of an ARB decision. In the last 25+ years, I have heard of only between five to ten cases where the chief appraiser appealed the value. The property owner has up to 60 days from receipt of the ARB hearing result (by the owner or his appointed agent) to file a judicial appeal. Binding arbitration must be filed within 45 days.

JUDICIAL APPEAL

The third and final step in the Texas property tax protest process, (other than any appeals), includes three options: 1) judicial appeals, 2) binding arbitration and 3) State Office of Administrative Hearings.

To provide perspective on the number of properties and appeals in Texas, consider the following data, compiled by the Texas Comptroller for the tax year 2016:

Total number of tax parcels in Texas	19,207,001	

Total number of protests	1,579,386	8%
Informal settlements	923,246	
Appraisal review board hearings / formal	338,630	
Judicial appeals (lawsuit in district court)	10,716	0.06% of all tax parcels
Binding arbitration filings	11,102	0.06% of all tax parcels
State Office of Administrative appeals	59	

A judicial appeal, binding arbitration or The State Office of Administrative Hearings (SOAH) is the third and final step in the protest process. Very few protest hearings result in a judicial appeal. For example, there were over 382,555 protests in Harris County in 2016 but only 4,492 judicial appeals. Only eight percent (8%) of assessed values are protested and 0.06% of tax parcels are litigated in Texas.

The Harris County number of appeals is high relative to the statewide average, based on Texas Comptroller data for tax year 2015. The statewide average in 2016 was 8% percent of assessed values protested versus 24% for Harris County. The volume of judicial appeals in Harris County was also higher: 27 judicial appeals per 10,000 properties versus 3.5 per 10,000 properties for the balance of the state, according to data provide by the Texas Comptroller of Public

Accounts. Harris County Appraisal District had 4,223 judicial appeals in 2015.

 PRACTICE TIP–If you own a commercial property valued at more than $1 million, and you have an appraisal review board hearing, you are likely paying about 10% more taxes than necessary by not continuing with a judicial appeal.

If you own a house worth more than $500,000, and you have an ARB hearing, you should seriously consider binding arbitration, particularly if your home is valued in excess of market value.

OPTIONS FOR JUDICIAL APPEALS

 PRACTICE TIP–The question should not be whether to appeal an ARB decision, but, instead, Why Not?

Most property owners choose one of two options for judicial appeals: 1) hire a law firm or 2) hire a tax consultant to coordinate the process. The decision should include consideration of the entire appeals process.

In general terms, the appeals process includes the

administrative appeals (informal and ARB) and the judicial appeals or binding arbitration. In the author's opinion, the best option is to maximize the results at each step. Results vary by county, but there are firms that compete effectively and generate meaningful reductions in the administrative hearing process, perhaps 10%. There are other firms that generate only token reductions in the administrative hearing process.

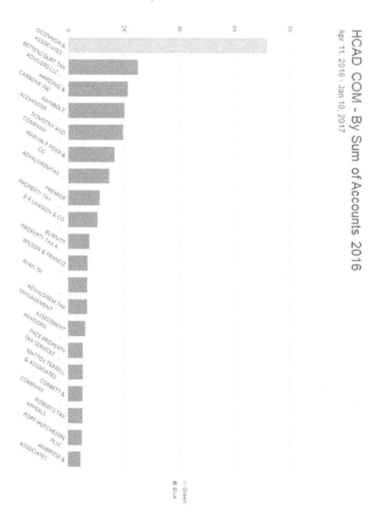

HCAD COM - By Sum of Accounts 2016

Apr 11, 2016 - Jan 10, 2017

The primary issue to ask is, "Is it possible to reduce taxes in a cost effective manner by continuing the appeals process to the judicial appeal or the binding arbitration phase?" Having more information on these processes will likely help you to make an informed decision.

A judicial appeal is a lawsuit in state district court. You can request either a bench trial or a jury trial. However, only a small portion of judicial appeals go to trial, less than one percent (1%). An issue to consider when deciding to file a judicial appeal is the potential tax savings versus the costs. Property owners should have a candid discussion with their property tax professional regarding their objectives and preferences with regard to fees. In my experience, over 95% of clients prefer a contingency fee approach. As long as they do not have to take a risk, they want to proceed. That is fine with us. We have coordinated and resolved over 20,000 lawsuits for property tax clients.

Other fee options are a flat fee and an hourly fee. There is a typical amount of work and expense attached to hiring attorneys and expert witnesses. Coordinating the filing of a property tax judicial appeal is typical for properties valued at $1 million and higher. Based on this, it is possible to price based on a flat fee. My experience is that clients prefer the contingency, but we are fine with either.

The final cost approach is based on an hourly fee for the attorney plus the expert witness fees. When clients receive savings of $500,000, $1 million or higher, they will veer away from the contingency fee approach. This approach reduces the maximum fees, but may or may not get the best result. It is really difficult to say. The same few people have been handling tax appeals for high-value parcels in many counties so it is difficult to determine if their approach is the best.

Binding arbitration is also an option for appeal after the appraisal review board. It is discussed later in the book.

State Office of Administrative Hearings (SOAH) – it is also possible to file an appeal after the appraisal review board with SOAH. However, since there were only 59 SOAH appeals out of 19 million parcels, SOAH appeals will not be addressed.

***

Now that you know exactly how the protest process works, we will review the steps for preparing a successful protest.

Chapter 10: Introduction To Market Value; The Basis For Most Property Tax Protests

In general, protests of assessed property value are based on a *market value concept or a uniform and equal value concept*. **Market value** protests rely on information that the market value is less than the assessed value or, less commonly, they compare the market value of the fee simple estate versus the leased fee estate.

The following are definitions for fee simple estate and leased fee estate from *The Dictionary of Real Estate Appraisal*, 6th edition:

"*Fee simple estate*. Absolute ownership unencumbered by any other interest or estate, subject only to the limitations imposed by the governmental powers of taxations, eminent, police power, and escheat."

"*Leased fee estate*. An ownership interest held by a landlord with the rights of use and occupancy conveyed by lease to others. The rights of the lessor (the leased fee owner) and the leased fee are specified by contract

terms contained within the lease."

Simply stated, the fee simple estate is the value as though not encumbered by long-term leases, which could be either favorable or unfavorable. The leased fee estate is the value as affected by long-term leases.

Uniform and equal protests are based on claims that the property is assessed at a higher level than comparable properties, *even if the property is assessed for less than market value.* Although both concepts are feasible, the market value approach has been more frequently used, especially prior to changes in the Texas Property Tax Code in 1997. The remainder of this chapter will be devoted to a preliminary discussion of the market value approach while a more detailed discussion of the uniform and equal approach will be presented in Chapter 14.

MARKET VALUE PROTESTS

A market value protest is based on information that the assessed value of the subject property exceeds its market value. In simple terms, **market value is the price which a person would pay for a property in an arm's-length transaction.**

Market value can be determined using one of three approaches: the sales

comparison approach, the income approach, or *the cost approach.* The
next four chapters address in detail each one of these
approaches and explain which is most applicable to your type
of property. First, we need to look at some introductory
definitions of market value and how to perform a highest
and best use analysis.

MARKET VALUE DEFINITIONS

The Texas Property Code, 2017 edition, Section 23.01 (b)
defines market value as follows:

The market value of property shall be determined by the
application of generally accepted appraisal methods and
techniques. If the appraisal district determines the appraised
value of a property using mass appraisal standards, the mass
appraisal standards must comply with the Uniform Standards
of Professional Appraisal Practice. The same or similar
appraisal methods and techniques shall be used in appraising
the same or similar kinds of property. However, each
property shall be appraised based upon the individual
characteristics that affect the property's market value, and all
available evidence that is specific to the value of the property
shall be taken into account in determining the property's
market value.

This is a fairly typical definition of market value. The primary elements are an open market transaction with a reasonable marketing time, a knowledgeable buyer and seller, and neither the buyer nor the seller is in a position to take advantage of the other.

However, what is not typical is the section that reads: "If the appraisal district determines the appraised value of a property using mass appraisal standards, the mass appraisal standards must comply with the Uniform Standards of Professional Appraisal Practice. The same or similar appraisal methods and techniques shall be used in appraising the same or similar kinds of property."

When appraisal districts incorrectly value property in their mass appraisal process, the same incorrect valuation process should be used in valuing properties during the appeal process. This includes the informal, appraisal review board and judicial appeal/binding arbitration.

The following are several examples of transactions which would NOT be considered arm's-length sales:

The owner of a small industrial property decides to sell the property. He mentions his interest in selling to a friend, who says, "That's exactly what I need! I'll buy it if you finance 100 percent of the price at 2 percent interest." The seller agrees to sell the property for a market price with financing better than is commercially available.

The purchaser knows a road has been plotted through the seller's suburban acreage tract. The seller is not aware of plans to put a road through his property. The property has not been exposed to the open market. The buyer and seller negotiate a price which does not reflect knowledge of the proposed road.

The owner of a home has been transferred from Houston to Boston. His company does not have a relocation program. He is desperate to sell because he does not want to make mortgage payments on an empty house in Houston and does not want to rent the house for fear it will be damaged. He mentions to the prospective buyer that he is anxious to sell because of his plans to move to Boston. The buyer offers to buy the home and close quickly for a 15% discount from market price.

A purchaser is assembling 20 properties for a high-rise office building site. He has contracted to purchase 19 of the 20 properties. The owner of the 20th property is aware that the buyer has secured all of the other tracts and the owner is holding out for an above-market price. He is ultimately able to extract a price equal to ten times the market value.

143

All of the above are examples of situations that would not be arm's-length sales and where the effective sales price would not be indicative of market value.

The following is the definition of market value from *The Dictionary of Real Estate Appraisal*, 6th edition, published by the Appraisal Institute, the premier industry association for appraisers:

Market value is the most probable price, as of a specified date, in cash, or in terms equivalent to cash, or in other precisely revealed terms for which the specified property rights should sell after reasonable exposure in a competitive market under all conditions requisite to a fair sale, with the buyer and seller each acting prudently, knowledgeably and for self-interest, and assuming that neither is under undue duress.

The above definition is essentially the same as the definition in the Texas Property Tax Code.

A nontechnical definition of market value might be as follows:

The amount of money you can get for selling a property

**if allowed adequate time to market the property with
both the buyer and seller being knowledgeable about
the property and market conditions and where neither
the buyer nor seller is in a position to take advantage of
the other.**

In Texas, the assessed value is supposed to be equal to the
market value of the property. An exception here is if other
properties in the area are assessed for less than their market
value. Many states use an assessment level which is less than
100 percent. This makes the property tax process slightly
more complicated. For example, if a property has a market
value of $100,000 and is located in a state with a 60-percent
assessment ratio, the assessed value would be calculated by
multiplying the market value times the assessment ratio
($100,000 x 60%). Because Texas uses a 100-percent
assessment rate, the assessed value should be equal to market
value unless similar properties are assessed for less than
market value or in special cases such as agricultural and
timber exemptions.

Appraised value is often used interchangeably with
market value, taxable value, and CAD value.
Appraised value is not interchangeable; it is the
taxable value after considering various exemptions
and special types of valuation. Exemptions are
covered separately. In many areas, homeowners save
10% to 20% because of exemptions. The Freeport
exemption for inventory can be 100%; the owner of

145

$100 million of fast-moving inventory could pay no property taxes on inventory.

There are a variety of special types of valuation for agricultural use, timber, open space, and other exemptions. Going into detail for these is beyond the scope of this book. Feel free to call our commercial property tax experts at 713-375-4399 for a free consultation. We do have staff with extensive expertise in this area.

HIGHEST AND BEST USE ANALYSIS

Performing a highest and best use analysis is an essential element of performing an appraisal. The following are the definitions of highest and best use, highest and best use of land for a site as though vacant, and highest and best use of the property as improved from *The Dictionary of Real Estate Appraisal, 6th edition:*

Highest and best use is the reasonably probable and legal use of vacant land or an improved property, which is physically possible, appropriately supported, financially feasible, and that results in the highest value. The four criteria the highest and best use must meet are legal permissibility, physical possibility, financial feasibility, and maximum profitability.

Legal permissibility addresses the allowable uses of the property. For example, you could not put a used car business on a lot that is deed restricted as single-family nor could you put a house on a lot that is deed restricted or zoned for industrial use.

Physical possibility addresses the practical uses of the site. It is not physically possible to build a regional shopping mall on a 5,000-square-foot residential lot.

Financial feasibility addresses use which is financially justified. It would not be financially feasible to build a $100,000 house on a $5 million lot in downtown Dallas nor would it be financially feasible to build a 60-story high-rise Class A office building in an area without a commercial or residential base to support it.

Maximum profitability addresses the most productive use of a site if more than one use is legally permissible, physically possible, and financially feasible.

Highest and best use of land or site as though vacant. Among all reasonable, alternative uses, the use that yields the highest present land value, after payments are made for labor, capital, and coordination. The use of a property based on the assumption that the parcel of land is vacant or can be made vacant by demolishing

147

any improvements. This analysis should also reflect the risk of each option. There are different levels of risk for a high-rise hotel, office building, and parking garage.

Appraisers often perform a highest and best use of land analysis as though vacant for improved properties. The highest and best use of a site **as though vacant** may be different from the improvements on a site. For example, the highest and best use of a site in a prime office location may be to build a high-rise Class A office building. If the site is currently improved with a high-rise Class C building, it may not be financially feasible to demolish the existing improvements and build the ultimate highest and best use as though vacant. If the current property as improved is worth more than the site as vacant (less the cost to demolish the improvements), the existing improvements are the highest and best use as improved.

Highest and best use of property as improved... The use that should be made of a property as it exists. An existing property should be renovated or retained as is so long as it continues to contribute to the total market value of the property, or until the return from a new improvement would more than offset the cost of demolishing the existing building and constructing a new one.

This analysis should address the market value of the land as though vacant, the market value of the real property as improved and any financially feasible renovations or upgrade. The following examples will demonstrate why performing the highest and best use analysis is a crucial step in preparing for a property tax protest.

A full block of land in downtown Austin is worth $8 million. It is currently improved with a 40-year-old 40,000-square-foot Class C office building. The office building is in good condition, considering its age and elements of functional obsolescence. It is not financially feasible to cure the functional obsolescence of the office building, and the cost to demolish the office building is approximately $80,000. The value of the office building based on capitalizing its existing income is $4 million. In this case, the highest and best use of the property as improved is to demolish the building and sell the lot. (Since the improvements do not contribute to the value, they should be assessed for zero dollars or some nominal amount.)

A prime, full block in downtown Houston is improved with a 10-year-old, mid-rise Class B office building. The highest and best use of the site as though vacant would be to construct a high-rise Class A office building. The market value of the land, if vacant, is $8 million. The market value of the land and improvements is $20 million. Spending $1 million to upgrade the building would increase net operating income to 10 percent and increase the value of the building to $22 million. The highest and best use of the property as improved is to spend $1 million to renovate the building, which will increase its market value by $2 million to $22 million. (It does not make sense to demolish the improvements since the market value exceeds the value of the site less the cost to demolish the improvements.)

A 45-year-old, 3,000-square-foot home in a prime location in Highland Park, Dallas, is functionally obsolete. The kitchen is too small. It does not have a master bedroom or a master bathroom. In addition, the ceiling height is one foot less than current standards. If the property were purchased, it would be purchased for the land value less the cost of demolition. The home is in good condition and the couple living in it is completely satisfied with the utilitarian aspects of the home. From a technical perspective, the highest and best use is to demolish the home and sell the lot. (This property should be assessed for land value only, with perhaps a token amount for the improvements depending on sales data. The improvements actually reduce the market value due to the cost to demolish them.)

Due to inexperience and improper judgment, a novice industrial developer builds a 10-story warehouse in downtown Austin with a 12-foot eave height. He can lease the space for only one-third of the projected rental rate. The project is not a good candidate for conversion to either office or residential use for technical reasons. The existing net operating income of the building is zero dollars per year.

There is no clear reason that either the occupancy rate or
rental rate will increase in the foreseeable future. The value
of the lot as vacant is $4 million. The cost to demolish the
building is $400,000. Since the existing improvements are
functionally obsolete and cannot be converted to another
use, the highest and best use as improved is to demolish the
improvements and sell the land.

The highest and best use as improved for most properties is
the current use. A critical and creative analysis can often
provide insight into reasons the existing improvements are
not the highest and best use of the property as improved.
The central appraisal district's mass appraisal estimate of
market value is based on the assumption that the existing
improvements are the highest and best use unless they have
performed an individual analysis for the subject property and
determined that their property information is correct, their
cost model factors are correct, and their valuation model is
accurate.

PRACTICE TIP–*Performing this analysis may reveal
an obvious means to dramatically reduce the assessed value
of your property*. A highest and best use analysis is
particularly warranted for old properties in an
area with relatively high land values.

Before we continue our discussion of market value protests,

we need to take a look at the less common type of market value protest that is based on the market value of the fee simple estate versus the leased fee estate and is a technically complex issue. However, in the age of retailers destroyed by Amazon and other factors, the valuation of real estate with or without the credit enhancements of large corporations is still in dispute.

Incredibly, since intangible personal property is not taxable in any state (with the exceptions of bonds and other securities in one or more states), it is bizarre that appraisal districts continue to dispute that there is value imputed to real estate when there is a promise to make payments for ten or twenty years or more. However, at an International Association of Assessment Officers (IAAO) meeting in September 2017, attended by the author, assessors put together a strong and committed front to fight for value based on having a lease in place. During a one-hour session, four or five speakers danced around the issue of promises to pay and the benefit of a credit enhancement from a company like Walgreens. Instead, they commented that you need to compare like stores to like stores. So compare leased or occupied stores to other lease or occupied stores.

The author was incredulous that the IAAO speakers never addressed the value of credit enhancement for a 25-year-lease from a company like Walgreens. Instead, it is just another occupied store. The IAAO position is a store leased by Walgreens for 30 years is no different than a store lease by

Bill Bad Credit for 30 years. Now I agree the value of the fee simple real estate is the same. However, the property leased by Walgreens consists of two assets: 1) a stream of monthly payments over 30 years from a tenant with a perceived good credit, and 2) the value of the real estate at the end of the 30-year lease. Given the amount of discounting that occurs over 30 years, the residual value of the store has little present value. In addition, given the uncertainty with which cities and neighborhoods evolve, the store could be in a great or terrible location at the end of the lease. The primary value of the store, leased by Walgreens, is the promise to pay by Walgreens.

One of the arguments made by the assessor team is that the vacant stores are vacant because of poor location or their highest and best use has changed. That may be the case sometimes. But when over 500 Toys R Us stores are shut, it is hard to say that each of those sites is in a "bad location" or "no longer the highest and best use of the site".

First Walmart and now Amazon is changing the retail landscape. Real Estate is part of the process of creative destruction occurring in the capitalist system. Businesses that do not generate a sufficient return go out of business. It happens hundreds or thousands of times a day. Each case involves immense pain as a result of a failed business. Fortunately, in America, failing in business is a tradition. any of our greatest success stories, including Walt Disney, failed multiple times.

Large bankruptcies in 2016 included:

Sun Edison - $11.5 billion in assets

Peabody Energy Corporation - $11 billion in assets

LINN Energy - $10 billion

Arch Coal Inc. - $8.4 billion

Breitburn Energy Partners - $4.8 billion

Energy XXI Ltd. - $4.7 billion

Republic Airways Holdings - $3.5 billion

Halcon Resources Corporation - $1.8 billion

Paragon Offshore PLC - $3.3 billion

Sandridge Energy–$4.7 billion

Hanjin Shipping Co. Ltd–$5.4 billion

China Fishery Group Ltd–$2.6 billion

CHC Group–$2.3 billion

Dex Media–$1.3 billion

2016 Retail Bankruptcies and Store Closings Include:

Hancock Fabrics–$151 million in assets

Sports Authority–$1.1 billion in debt; 460 stores

Ventis–includes Eastern Mountain Sports, Bob's Stores and
Sport Chalet

Aéropostale–154 stores closed

Walmart: Closed 269 stores

Kmart/Sears: 78 stores closed

Ralph Lauren: Closed at least 50 stores

Macy's revealed plans to close down 100 stores in early 2017

However, some of the creative destruction occurs in public
view.   It is still painful and it affects many people. The
following is a list of retail bankruptcies in 2017:

The Limited	Hhgregg
Wet Seal	Radio Shack
Eastern Outfitters	Gordman Stores
Max Azria	Gander Mountain
Vanity	Payless ShoeSource

O'Connor Tax Reduction Experts 713.369.5958

Rue 21

Gymboree

Papaya Clothing

True Religion
Apparel

Alfred Angelo

Perfumania

Vitamin World

Aerosoles

Toys R Us

FOUR ISSUES THAT THE ASSESSORS DID NOT ADDRESS

The assessors discussion was important more for what it did not address than for what it did address: 1) assessors did not address the business enterprise value and pricing differential for a real estate lease guaranteed by a public company versus by a single-location operator, 2) the canard that vacant stores are vacant because they are a poor location, 3) the impact of a dark PO Box on the shadow retail (adjacent shopping center), 4) the impact of deed restrictions on occupied stores, and 5) empirical data.

This is the second presentation the author has seen on this topic in two months. The first one was at the Texas A&M Legal Conference in San Antonio in August 2017. At the A&M conference, the presenter, for a lower value, presented data on about 100 sales and made a strong case that the value of the property without the promise to pay by a creditworthy lessee is perhaps only 20% to 40% of the value with credit enhancement by the tenant. Hence, 60% to 80% of retail owned and leased by major companies has a tendency to be overvalued until they sell it. And then there is proof of value. The speaker for the appraisal district side was articulate and made his points, but he never addressed the intangible value of the lease. The intangible personal property, such as a contract or a lease is not taxable in Texas or in any other state. However, assessors have decided to ignore the intangible value of the lease and attribute it to real estate.

Issue 1–Not Assessed By Assessors (IAAO September 2017 Conference) - Assessors did not address the business enterprise value and pricing differential for a real estate lease guaranteed by a public company versus by a single-location operator. As noted above, the only data presented and displayed has been from representatives of property owners, and the data has not been vetted by peer publishing to my knowledge. However, the results ring true to me.

I clearly remember doing a hearing for former Food Lion stores in Houston (Harris County Appraisal District). The discounts from the appraisal district's final value for the current year were in the range of 80% to 90%. Now in fairness to HCAD, they just valued the property on cost, not recognizing the external obsolescence. However, when Food Lion exited the market and buyers looked at sales at the stores, all the major players recognized the problem locations and passed on the sale. However, there are no bad properties; there are just bad prices. The market will move any property given reasonable exposure if the seller is willing to accept the judgment of the market. The corporate staff at Food Lion had no emotional attachments to these properties (at least not positive ones) and they were ready to mark to market and reduce the operating expenses.

Issue 2–The canard that vacant stores are vacant because they are a poor location.

There have been scores of bankruptcies affecting more than 100 retail locations. The assessor position is that only low-

quality locations fail. The quality of the sales at the store is
one of two possible factors: 1) can store operate profitably (if
some stores are being kept) and 2) is the contract rent below
or above market rent? There are problems with both these
hypotheses.

First concern–can the store operate profitably? Of course,
from an appraisal perspective, this is not the correct
approach. The correct approach is to evaluate whether the
current operation is the highest and best use of the site. It
may be that the location is profitable because of a twenty-five
year old lease with seventy-five years remaining. If it is
determined that a valuable leasehold estate exists, the next
step in the process is to evaluate the highest and best use of
the site. If the current contract rent is $2 per square foot
(PSF) and the market rent is $20 PSF, would the business be
profitable after paying market rent of $20 PSF? In this case,
the success or failure of the individual business is not
relevant. If the business is profitable at $2 rents and would
not be at $20 rents, the business is not financially feasible
when considering market rent.

However, if the contract rent is $20 and the market rent is
$10, it is possible the business would be financially feasible
with market rent but not with contract rent.

How many of the Radio Shack locations, often in-line in
shopping centers or malls, are "bad locations?" I'll

acknowledge that there are poorly picked locations. But there are many reasons locations can fail, including real estate location, management, inventory mix/product mix, lower-priced competition (Amazon) and more convenient competition (Amazon). Some locations are terrible and they generate low rents and sales prices for the second generation.

At the end of the day, the value of the real estate (without the intangible of the lease) is the amount for which it would sell, subject to any restrictions.

Issue 3–Deed restrictions in place at resold stores greatly diminish their value

Multiple speakers on a panel at the International Association of Assessment Officers (IAAO) suggested that a meaningful factor in the low sales prices for sales of retail and restaurant to second generation users was the deed restrictions put in place in the deed. Incorporating these same deed restrictions in acquisitions would provide a means to reduce taxes and not destroy any economic value if these provisions are routinely put in place upon sale.

Issue 4–Empirical Data

The IAAO analysis is internally flawed. See excerpts from their classification plan:

Investment Class A– "Buyers of investment class A big-PO Box retail properties typically are national investors, such as real estate investment trusts, insurance companies, and retirement funds, looking for newer improvements **with a creditworthy national or regional retail chain tenant under a long-term, generally triple-net lease."** Leased class A properties generally are subject to long-term leases and are purchased with significant years remaining on the lease.

Investment Class B–**Remaining lease terms** on these properties, while not as long as for investment class A properties**, generally exceed 10 years.**

Investment Class C–Remaining **lease terms are relatively short,** usually less than 10 years.

Investment Class D–They are **often vacant or soon-to-be-vacant properties** with a highest and best use for a second-generation use.

In other words, the assessors have discovered that new buildings with high-credit tenants with long-term leases sell for the most and vacant buildings sell for the least.

However, the tax assessors make no attempt to differentiate between real estate and intangible personal property. The value of a new building without a lease to a high-credit tenant may be below replacement cost.

Generally, the value for the fee simple estate is the value for the property, assuming that there are no long-term leases at either above-market or below-market rents. The market value of the leased fee estate is the market value based on existing long-term leases (typically considered longer than one year) at either above-market or below-market rental rates. If a property is encumbered by a long-term lease at a below-market rental rate, the value of leased fee estate will be less than the market value of the fee simple estate. If a property has long-term leases at above-market rental rates, the value of the leased fee estate will exceed the market value of the fee simple estate.

In addition, and equally important, the market value of the fee simple estate DOES NOT include the value of credit enhancement by Walgreens agreeing to a long-term lease. If there is a credit enhancement that occurs because of the lessee's promise to pay, it should not be included in the value of the property for the fee simple real estate. However, this was not one of the issues addressed by IAAO assessors valuing retail with particular emphasis on how to differentiate between vacant and occupied stores, at the September 2017 Annual Conference.

The value for the fee simple real estate should consider:

The market value for rent not limiting the use to the current tenant and

The market value of the property based on market rent and not including any benefit of the credit of the tenant.

Sample Triple Net Property for Sale

Property Address:	Midland, TX
Square Feet:	14,820 SF
Sales Price:	$8,191,100 (asking)
Price per Square Foot (SF):	$552.02
Implied Value of the Property at end	$61.25
Total Rent Payments over 17 years of the property life	$7,657,803(89% of payments)
Residual Value Based on 5.5% yield	$ 907,725 (11% of payments)

This investment is being sold on a 5.5% yield. However, the IRR based on the rental payments and selling the property for $61.25 is only about 0.5%. The IRR increases to 10% if the residual sales price is increased to $1,600 per square foot.

The proportion of the total payments derived from rent versus from the residual value (sales price at the end of the lease) illustrates that almost all of the value depends on the credit enhancement provided by Walgreens. To say there is no difference between a building leased by Walgreens and a tenant with no credit or bad credit is preposterous.

Consider the following:

IF LONG-TERM LEASES ARE:	MARKET VALUE OF FEE SIMPLE ESTATE WILL BE:
Below Market Rent	More than Market Value of Leased Fee Estate
Above Market Rent	Less than Market Value of Leased Fee Estate

* * *

Let's proceed to a discussion of the more common approaches to estimating market value.

Chapter 11: Three Approaches For Estimating Market Value

The three primary approaches to estimating market value in the appraisal profession are the **sales comparison, income, and cost approaches.** This chapter will discuss which approaches are most applicable for most types of properties. *The objective is to help you ensure that you spend your time on the approach which will receive primary consideration at the property tax hearing.* Each of the approaches to estimating market value is discussed in detail in the next three chapters.

SINGLE-FAMILY (HOUSES, TOWNHOMES, AND CONDOS)

The **sales comparison approach** is the primary appraisal methodology used at hearings for single-family houses. Artfully employing the sales comparison approach is typically the basis for reducing the assessed value of a home at a property tax hearing. (For the sake of simplicity, we will refer to all single-family dwellings as houses. The applications for houses also apply to townhomes, cooperatives, and condominiums.) If you have limited time to prepare for a hearing and are not certain which appraisal approach to utilize, focus on preparing the sales comparison approach. If the house is less than two or three years old, it is important to value the property using sales of previously occupied homes. If the assessed value is more than the purchase price of the land plus the total cost of improvements (or the amount you paid to purchase the house), the cost approach would be helpful.

The income approach is not typically used for single-family houses, except in the case of less expensive homes, perhaps $125,000 and lower. These houses are sometimes bought as rental properties. Most houses which are valued above $125,000 are bought as primary residences and not for use as rental property. However, about 20 percent, approximately 14 million houses are owned by investors.

The cost approach is not typically used for property tax hearings for single-family houses. An exception would be fairly new houses. In these cases, the appraisal district will often attempt to limit the information considered at the hearing to the purchase price of the land, plus the actual construction costs of the improvements. The purchase price of the land and cost of improvements can be more than or less than market value.

RAW LAND OR VACANT LAND

The **sales comparison approach** is the primary approach used for valuing raw land. The cost approach is not applicable since raw land, by definition, does not include improvements. The income approach may be applicable to valuing raw land. For example, the land is sometimes used to derive income from parking or is leased on a long-term basis to a developer who builds improvements. However, the vast majority of property tax hearings for raw land improvements focus on the sales comparison approach.

SINGLE–FAMILY SUBDIVISIONS

All three approaches can be used to value a single-family subdivision (a collection of single-family lots which have not yet been improved with houses).

The **cost approach** is applied by calculating the market value of the land plus the cost of improvements and an allowance for entrepreneurial profit (less any depreciation, if applicable).

The **income approach** is applied by performing a discounted cash flow analysis to calculate the present value of revenues less expenses.

The **sales comparison approach** can be used to calculate the retail market value (market value of a single lot) of the lots being sold when performing a discounted cash flow analysis. The sales comparison approach can also be used to estimate the market value based on bulk sales of groups of lots similar to the subject lots. The approach used will vary by the appraisal district.

COMMERCIAL INCOME PROPERTIES

Commercial income properties include apartments, shopping centers, warehouse buildings, office buildings, and other types of commercial income properties.

The two primary approaches to value utilized at property tax hearings for income properties are the **income** and **sales comparison approaches**. The income approach is generally emphasized. The cost approach is not typically used unless the improvements are less than two to three years old.

OWNER-OCCUPIED COMMERCIAL PROPERTY

The **sales comparison approach** is the primary appraisal methodology at property tax hearings for owner-occupied commercial buildings. The ultimate use of many of these properties involves both a real estate and a business enterprise component. It can be difficult to separate the business enterprise value of a successful business from the market value of the real estate.

The most important and challenging portion of property tax appeals is for commercial property that also includes intangible value. This includes hotels, self-storage, apartments, and real estate leased by the tenant with good credit. Real estate is just the land and improvements. It does not include the value from leases, which are intangible.

CONCLUSION

If there is sufficient time, prepare an appraisal analysis for the sales comparison, income, and cost approaches for your property tax hearing. In addition, also perform a uniform and equal analysis. You can present evidence in the order which benefits your case. In other words, start with the approach to value which supports the lowest market value for the property. If the appraiser for the central appraisal district does not agree to the value you have proposed, you can then present evidence from a second or third approach to value. Follow the information in the next three chapters to build your case.

Chapter 12: Sales Comparison Approach

The sales comparison approach allows you to estimate market value by comparing your property to similar properties which recently sold or are listed for sale and as stated in the prior chapter is the approach most commonly used for single-family homes. Start building your case by gathering information on comparable sales. The highest and best use of the comparable sales should be similar to the highest and best use for the subject property when considering location, year built, size, quality, and appeal. Search for sales which occurred up to 12 to 15 months before the valuation date (January 1 of the tax year.) Although there is no technical reason not to use sales which occur after the valuation date, some appraisal district staffs refuse to consider sales which occur after that time. You may need to use comparable sales which are one to four years old, depending on the type of property and level of sales activity.

Sources of comparable sales include appraisers, real estate brokers, Realtors™, and data services. The central appraisal district may also provide information on comparable sales.

PRACTICE TIP–Texas law requires you file a property tax protest to get comparable sales data from the appraisal district. Filing a property tax protest annually provides you with data to better understand the value of your property and the option of attending the property tax protest hearing. You do not have to attend the property tax hearing if you can't find evidence to support a reduction using errors in their data, market value or unequal appraisal.

Gather comparable sales data, plot the subject property and the comparable sales on a map and summarize the key fields of data for the subject property and the comparable sales on a single sheet of paper. In other words, summarize information that prospective buyers would consider. Depending on the quality and quantity of data available, select 3 to 10 comparable sales to inspect for consideration as final comparable sales. Ideally, you should select 7 to 10 comparable sales to inspect for consideration as final comparables.

After inspecting the subject property, perform a drive-by inspection of selected comparables. Take notes regarding the physical attributes of the comparable sales and the surrounding properties. Take several photographs of each comparable property, including one from the front and one from an oblique angle. Compile any information missing from your summary of the comparable sales.

Sources of additional information regarding the comparable sales could include the seller, current owner, broker, or central appraisal district records.

 PRACTICE TIP–Inspecting and taking photographs of the comparable properties will provide you with more information than an appraisal district has available. This should position you as more knowledgeable and credible at the hearing.

The next step is to select the best comparable sales. From a technical appraisal perspective, these are the sales which are most similar to the subject property. *From a practical perspective, the best sales to prepare for a property tax hearing are those which have the lowest sales prices but are generally similar in appearance and attributes to the subject property.*

An excellent tool for selecting the best comparable sales is to prepare a hand-written summary of the basic physical attributes for the subject property and the probable comparable sales after your drive-by inspection. Fields of data which may be incorporated into this summary include the date of sale, property size (in square feet or units), year of construction, property class for multifamily (A, B, C, or D), street address, sales price per unit or square foot, and condition. When reviewing the subject property, make note of any **deferred maintenance**, the result of not performing routine repairs or replacing items such as roofs or air conditioning/heating systems.

The unit of measure for properties varies depending on the type of property. Most properties are valued via the sales comparison approach based on a square foot measure. Apartments are often valued using a per-unit basis while hotels and motels are valued on a per-room basis, and car washes, garages, and oil change facilities on a per-bay basis. Churches and theaters can be valued based on the number of seats.

Select the best comparable sales for the property tax protest hearing based on reviewing your photographs of the subject property, possible comparables, and the summary of data for the possible comparables.

DERIVING A CONCLUSION

The final step in performing the sales comparison approach for a property tax hearing is to determine a market value based on the data.

Options for determining a final value via the sales comparison approach for a property tax hearing could include a grid analysis, ranking, or analysis based on the best one or two comparable sales.

A **grid analysis** takes into account and makes adjustments for many factors. A sample grid analysis appears on the next page.

In a technically correct fee appraisal, adjustments are typically made for real property rights conveyed, financing, conditions of sale, market conditions, economic characteristics, location, physical condition, size and marketability, quality, and appeal, among other adjustments. *For the purpose of preparing for a property tax hearing, a reasonable compromise is to make subjective adjustments for location, physical condition, size, and quality/appeal.*

The unadjusted sales price (using the appropriate unit of measure such as per square foot) for each of the comparable sales is listed at the top of the grid. Adjustments for each of the listed items are shown on the grid. The net sum of the adjustments is totaled near the bottom of the grid. The indicated value for the subject property is calculated by multiplying the unadjusted sales price (for each sale) times 100 percent plus the total net adjustments. See the lines "Sales Price PSF," "Total Net Adjustments," and "Adjusted Value" in the grid analysis. For example, the "Adjusted Value" for sale #2 is calculated as follows:

174

$43.50 x (100% - 5%) = $41.33

The comparable sales are adjusted to the level of the subject property. A positive adjustment is made for properties which have an inferior attribute to bring that property up to the level of the subject property. Properties which have a superior attribute are adjusted downward to bring them down to the level of the subject property. The following sample adjustment grid shows how several comparable properties might be compared to the subject property.

SAMPLE ADJUSTMENT GRID

Sale#	Subject	1	2	3	4	5
Location	Average	Average	Good	Average	Fair	Average
Condition	Average	Good	Average	Good	Average	Fair
Size	10,000	20,000	15,000	5,000	10,000	8,000
Quality/Appeal	Good	Good	Good	Average	Average	Fair
Sales Price/PSF	N/A	$40.00	$43.50	$45.00	$31.50	$30.00

ADJUSTMENTS

Location	0%	-10%	0%	10%	0%
Condition	-10%	0%	-10%	0%	10%
Size	10%	5%	-10%	0%	0%
Quality/Appeal	0%	0%	10%	10%	20%
Total					
Net Adjustments	0%	-5%	-10%	20%	30%
Adjusted Value	$40.00	$41.33	$40.50	$37.80	$39.00

Range of Adjusted Values	$37.80 - $41.33
Mean	$39.73
Mid-point	$39.56
2 Sales with the least net adjustment	1($40.00) and 2 ($41.33)

Chapter 12, Table 1

One of the first questions asked about the sales comparison approach is how the subjective adjustments are performed. My answer: it is a combination of judgment, experience, and common sense. For example, for the quality and appeal adjustment in the sample grid, you must decide whether a building with good appeal would sell for $4 more a square foot than a building with average appeal. If so, a 10-percent upward adjustment is appropriate to bring the average quality/appeal building up to the level of the good quality/ appeal building. From a technical fee appraisal analysis viewpoint, the adjustment process is more complicated than this brief explanation indicates. However, reasonable judgments grounded in common sense are sufficient for a property tax protest hearing.

The size adjustment is based on differences in size between the subject property and the comparable sales based on the premise that larger buildings typically sell for a lower per-square-foot price than smaller buildings. In addition, larger buildings are less expensive to build (on a per-square-foot basis). Smaller buildings receive a downward adjustment to bring their sales price down to the level of the subject property. Larger buildings receive an upward adjustment to bring their sales price up to the level of the subject property. Use common sense and a test of reasonableness when applying adjustments. Consider the absolute dollar difference between the subject property and the comparable sales when applying a percentage adjustment. After you have finished applying the percentage adjustments, review the adjusted values for the comparable sales. They should form a fairly tight range. The adjusted value of the highest comparable sale should not exceed the adjusted value of the lowest comparable sale by more than 20 percent.

If there is a large range of value in the comparable sales after making adjustments, it indicates that either: 1) the data is not accurate, 2) the adjustment is not correct or 3) there is an error in the valuation methodology.

Reaching a final opinion of value via the sales comparison approach involves a combination of art and science. Reviewing the range, mean, and mid-point of adjusted values provides guidance to the final value for the sales comparison approach. Also consider which comparable sales needed the least net adjustment. In the above grid, sales 1 and 2 needed the least net adjustments. This indicates that they were the most similar to the subject property.

Place additional emphasis on sales which require less adjustment when determining to a final value for the subject property. In the above example, a final value of $40.50 per square foot is a reasonable final opinion of value for the subject property via the sales comparisons based on sales 1 and 2, which required the least net adjustment.

A **ranking system** is another method to arrive at an opinion of value via the sales comparison approach. To use the ranking method, rank the comparable sales and the subject property in order of desirability. After you rank the comparable sales and the subject property in order of desirability, review the sales price per square foot (or use another unit of comparison) to see if they generally increase or decrease in value with the desirability of the properties.

If the unadjusted sales prices per square foot do not increase with your ranking of property desirability, your evaluation is inconsistent with the market or the data is incorrect. After you are comfortable with your ranking of comparable sales and the subject property, review the one or two sales which are more desirable and less desirable than the subject property. The final value conclusion should be in between the unadjusted sales prices for the properties which are slightly more desirable and slightly less desirable than the subject property.

RANKING ANALYSIS EXAMPLE

	Unadjusted Sales Price
Sale 5	$30.00
Sale 4	$31.50
Subject	N/A
Sale 1	$40.00
Sale 2	$43.50
Sale 3	$45.00

This ranking analysis indicates the subject property is superior to sale four and similar/inferior to sale 1. This brackets the value conclusion between $31.50 and $40.00 per square foot.

Chapter 12, Table 2

Focusing your analysis on the **best one or two sales** can be an effective approach when there are a limited number of good comparable sales. For example, if you have 15 comparable sales but only 1 or 2 which are highly similar to the subject property, focusing your analysis on the best sales may be the most effective approach. Use a combination of a grid analysis and/or a ranking analysis to determine an opinion of value for the subject property based on the best comparable sales. A ranking analysis is not used often at property tax hearings.

 PRACTICE TIP–While a ranking analysis is not used often at property tax hearings, it is a compelling means to make your case. If you can convince the appraiser or appraisal review board that several sales are inferior to the subject property (and have a lower price per square foot (PSF) and that several are superior with a higher price PSF, you should prevail. Photographs can be helpful.

Multiply your conclusion of market value per square foot for the subject property by the number of square feet in the subject property to reach a final value in the sales comparison approach.

Finally, a word about appraising raw land, which is probably the most difficult type of property to appraise since most land appraisals are done using only the sales comparison approach. The cost approach is not appropriate because raw land, by definition, has no buildings on it. The income approach is not appropriate unless the land is used in some way to generate income. Thus, it is necessary to rely on the sales comparison approach, which entails research to locate information on sales of similar properties. Typically, adjustments are made to the comparable properties (based on their per-square-foot or per-acre sales price) to bring them up or down to the level of the subject property. Negative adjustments are applied to the comparable sales for attributes which are superior to the subject property; upward adjustments are applied to the comparable sales price for attributes which are inferior to the subject property

APPLICABILITY OF THE SALES COMPARISON APPROACH FOR A PROPERTY TAX PROTEST

Comparing the final value via the sales comparison approach for the subject property with the current assessed value **estimated** by the central appraisal district indicates whether the sales comparison approach will be helpful in reducing your property taxes. If the sales comparison approach indicates a market value less than the assessed value, it should be useful in reducing your property taxes. If the sales comparison approach indicates a market value higher than your current assessed value, it would not be prudent to present this information at the property tax hearing.

Chapter 13: Income Approach

The income approach is based on the premise that investors purchase income properties for their perceived income stream. Investors focus on the perceived present value of future income stream which can be derived from the subject property. A property which had excellent actual income in the past but has no expectation of future income may have a low value. For example, apartments near an Army base which has been ordered closed may become essentially worthless if there is no other nearby economic activity which will generate tenants for the apartment complex.

The income approach is used predominately for income properties and would not typically be applied to single-family residences and owner-occupied commercial properties (for appealing property taxes). The income approach can be most accurately applied to properties which are in good condition, are subject to arms-length leases, and are operated by skilled property managers.

Small differences in key assumptions cause significant changes in the final value conclusion when performing the income approach. The contract rental rates for a property subject to long-term leases may be greater than or lesser than market rent. A property operated by an inexperienced property manager may have a higher vacancy and above-market expenses. A property operated by a cash-strapped real estate investor may have below-market expenses, below-market rents, and deferred maintenance. Performing an accurate income approach analysis exceeds the capacity of some semi-active real estate investors. The result of a combination of minor changes in income approach assumptions is illustrated in this chapter.

The following is a sample income analysis which incorporates the major elements of performing the income approach:

Sample Income Analysis

Sierra Pines Apartments

(100 Units; 80,000 Net Rentable Square Feet)

Potential Gross Income ($0.60 PSF per month)	$576,000
Less Vacancy (10%)	-57,600
Plus Other Income ($100 per unit per year)	10,000
Effective Gross Income	**$528,400**
Expenses	
General Operating Expense	$320,000
Replacement Reserves ($275 per unit)	27,500
Leasing Commission (N/A)	0
Management Fee (6%)	31,704
Tenant Improvements (N/A)	0
Total Expenses	**$379,204**
Net Operating Income	$149,196
Divided by Capitalization Rate	8%
Market Value via the Income Approach	$1,864,950

Chapter 13, Table I

POTENTIAL GROSS INCOME

Potential gross income is the rental income which could be generated if the subject property were 100 percent leased at market rent and all tenants paid their rent.

The potential gross income for the leased fee estate is often different from the potential gross income for the fee simple estate. In Texas, an appraisal performed for property tax purposes should focus on the fee simple estate. The rents used when calculating the value via the fee simple estate should be market rents instead of contract rents. Contract rents should be used when calculating the market value of the leased fee estate. For practical purposes, many property owners use contract rents for market rents if the contract rents are less than market rents. They also argue that market rents should be used if contract rents exceed market rents. (See Chapter 10 for an explanation of the difference between the fee simple estate and the leased fee estate.)

VACANCY

Market vacancy should be utilized when performing an income approach for the fee simple estate. Even though a single-tenant building may be 100-percent occupied, the market vacancy should be deducted when performing the income approach since the building is unlikely to be 100-percent occupied for the balance of its economic life. Even if a lease with an excellent credit tenant provides for an income stream 50 years into the future, use market vacancy when performing the income analysis of the fee simple estate.

 PRACTICE TIP–Using market vacancy is not intuitive and is particularly important for property taxes. This again ties to the critical issue of valuing property using the fee simple estate instead of the leased fee estate.

Actual vacancy should be considered (during the term of the lease) when performing an analysis of the leased fee estate. The analysis of the leased fee estate is not applicable to property tax valuations in Texas.

OTHER INCOME

Other income could include items such as forfeited deposits, tenant reimbursements for common area expenses, vending income, late fees, and other miscellaneous income. It is important to review other income for revenue that is not related to recurring operations. Refunds for property tax litigation, litigation settlements for other purposes, insurance payments for damages and capital contributions are sometimes included in the income statements. However, owners prepare income and expense statements in many formats. Carefully scrutinize the other income which is not related to the real estate.

Sales of items such as PO Boxes and truck rental should not be considered as part of the income for a self-storage facility. Of course, the related expenses should also be excluded.

It is unclear whether other income is real estate income. Any revenue not related to the use of real estate should be scrutinized.

EFFECTIVE GROSS INCOME

Effective gross income is equal to potential gross income less vacancy plus other income.

Effective Gross Income = Potential Gross Income - Vacancy + Other Income.

GENERAL OPERATING EXPENSES

General operating expenses as discussed in this chapter are all expenses other than replacement reserves, leasing commissions, management fees, and tenant improvements. You may need to consult with your accountant or an appraiser regarding all types of expenses incurred for your particular type of income property.

For appraisal purposes, depreciation, interest, and

amortization are not operating expenses. Exclude depreciation, interest, and amortization for valuations for property taxes and financing.

When performing an income approach for property tax purposes, consider actual expenses, market expenses, and expenses considered appropriate by the appraisal district. Actual expenses are those reported by the owner. They can be above or below market expenses. Sources of market data include Institute of Real Estate Management (IREM), Building Owners and Managers Association (BOMA), and data vendors. Operating expenses allowed by the appraisal district should be considered for a variety of reasons.

Expenses allowed by the appraisal district may exceed actual expenses. In this case, use the appraisal district expense allowance instead of actual expenses.

Actual expenses may be higher than appraisal district expenses due to errors made by the appraisal district, mismanagement or by including capital expenditures in operating expenses. Routine appraisal district errors regarding expenses include not accurately indicating whether tenants are reimbursed for operating expenses and not considering the cost of utilities for master-metered apartments.

Compare your actual expenses to the appraisal district expenses and be prepared to discuss the reason for any material differences at the appeal hearing.

REPLACEMENT RESERVE

Replacement reserve is an allowance to replace property components which have an economic life shorter than the life of the structure. This includes items such as roofs, parking lots, carpeting, air conditioner, and appliances.

LEASING COMMISSIONS

Leasing commissions reflect the economic cost to procure tenants. For office buildings, retail centers, and warehouse buildings, owners typically use outside leasing agents. For apartment projects, the cost of leasing is typically included as part of the general operating expenses. The exception is apartment owners often pay apartment locators a leasing commission; typically one to three month's rent.

If a commercial property is leased by the owner, it is appropriate to make an allowance for leasing commissions when performing the income approach. The time spent by the owner reflects an economic contribution. A possible purchaser may or may not perform the leasing function. To calculate the economic value of the real estate aside from the owner's contribution to operating it, the market cost of leasing the subject property should be included in the operating expenses. Leasing costs vary from 3 to 10 percent of effective gross rental income depending primarily on the size, location, and the number of tenants. Including an allowance for the cost of leasing, even if the owner does all leasing, is typical and routine.

MANAGEMENT FEE

The management fee is an allowance to hire a management company to operate the subject property. Management fees vary based on the size, quality, and type of property. They range from a low of perhaps 2 percent for large properties up to 8 or 10 percent for small properties. Even if the owner personally manages the subject property, it is appropriate for professional appraisers who perform appraisals for banks to include an allowance for a management fee in the operating expenses.

TENANT IMPROVEMENTS

Tenant improvements reflect the cost of refinishing space for new or existing tenants. This typically includes items such as floor coverings, painting and moving interior walls, and a variety of enhancements and high levels of finish. For larger spaces (in excess of 10,000 square feet), the cost of tenant improvements is substantial for each new tenant.

Tenant improvements are typically included in the general operating expenses for apartments but are separated for warehouse, retail, and office buildings. Tenant improvements are typically low for industrial buildings, are somewhat higher for retail buildings, and are generally a significant expense for office buildings. Tenant improvements can also be a major expense when converting a retail building from one type of tenant to another. For example, converting a grocery store space to general retail use may cost $15 to $40 per square foot. Tenant improvements are routinely high in medical/professional buildings, based on the construction of small treatment rooms, many of which have plumbing and specialized fixtures.

Tenant improvements should be reflected in the income analysis (even if they did not occur during the previous year) if they are routinely incurred at the subject property type. This amount can be estimated by multiplying the cost to hire vendors to perform the work (on a per-square-foot basis) times the number of square feet refurbished in a typical year.

TOTAL OPERATING EXPENSES

This is the total of the above-listed expenses (general operating expenses, replacement reserve, leasing commissions, management fee, and tenant improvements).

NET OPERATING INCOME

Net operating income is the effective gross income less the total operating expenses.

Net Operating Income = Effective Gross Income – Total Operating Expenses.

CAPITALIZATION RATE

The capitalization rate is used to convert the net operating income into an indicated value for the subject property. It is effectively a conversion rate. Capitalization rates vary, depending on the type, class (A, B, or C), age, location, occupancy, and condition of the property. Economic conditions and capital market trends also influence capitalization rates. You can obtain information on capitalization (cap) rates by contacting appraisers or real estate brokers. Cap rates are calculated by dividing net operating income (NOI) by the sales price for recently sold similar properties.

Many readers may be more familiar with the price earnings ratio (PE ratio) used for stocks. The PE is the price divided by the earnings. The capitalization rate is the reciprocal of the PE ratio.

Capitalization Rate = Net Operating Income ÷ Market Value (aka Price)

Price Earnings Ratio = Price / Earning (aka Net Operating Income)

MARKET VALUE

The market value is calculated by dividing the net operating income by the capitalization rate.

Market Value = Net Operating Income/Capitalization Rate

* * *

The first step in performing the income approach is to gather the necessary data. This includes rent comparables and data on vacancy, other income, expense comparables, market data regarding replacement reserves, leasing commissions, management fees, tenant improvements, and capitalization rates.

Possible sources of data for preparing the income approach include real estate appraisers, brokers, investors, data providers, and the central appraisal district. The process of gathering adequate data to perform an income analysis will likely take more time than performing the income analysis.

 PRACTICE TIP–Most appraisal districts have either manuals or other printed material that explains their routine for performing the income approach. For example, Harris County Appraisal District annually generates a report with metrics for valuation organized by property type and location. Call or send an open records request to your appraisal district to see what they have available.

However, the income approach may be well worth the time you invest in it. The following analysis shows the sensitivity of this approach:

PROPERTY VALUE ANALYSIS

PROPERTY:	ANYWHERE APARTMENTS		
LOCATION:			
ACCT. NO.	CASE - A		
NET RENTABLE S. F. :	80,000		
UNITS	100		

	Annual PSF	monthly psf	
GROSS INCOME	$9.60	$0.80	$768,000
OTHER INCOME			$10,000
TOTAL POTENTIAL GROSS INCOME			$778,000
LESS STABILIZED VACANCY	10.0%		$76,800
EFFECTIVE GROSS INCOME			**$701,200**
FIXED EXPENSES - INSURANCE	$0.00		$0
VARIABLE EXPENSES	$6.25		$500,000
OTHER OPERATING			
MANAGEMENT	6.00%		$42,072
RESERVES FOR REPLACEMENTS	$350.00		$35,000
TENANT IMPROVEMENTS	$0.00		$0
LEASING COM.	0.00%		$0
TAXES			$0
TOTAL EXPENSES			**$577,072**
NET OPERATING INCOME			**$124,128**
CAP RATE			8.5%
MARKET VALUE			**$1,460,329**

Income Attributed to Vacancy and Concessions

SENSITIVITY ANALYSIS OF INCOME APPROACH

PROPERTY:			ANYWHERE APARTMENTS		
LOCATION:					
ACCT. NO.			**CASE - B**		
NET RENTABLE S. F. :					**80,000**
UNITS					100
annual psf			monthly psf		
GROSS INCOME		$9.84		$0.82	$787,200
OTHER INCOME					$12,500
TOTAL POTENTIAL GROSS INCOME					$799,700
LESS STABILIZED VACANCY			8.00%		$62,976
EFFECTIVE GROSS INCOME					**$736,724**
FIXED EXPENSES - INSURANCE			$0.00		$0
VARIABLE EXPENSES			$5.75		$460,000
OTHER OPERATING					
MANAGEMENT			4.00%		$29,469
RESERVES FOR REPLACEMENTS			$325.00		$32,500
TENANT IMPROVEMENTS			$0.00		$0
LEASING COM.			0.00%		$0
TAXES					$0
TOTAL EXPENSES			$521,969	$	
NET OPERATING INCOME					**$214,755**
CAP RATE					7.50%

MARKET VALUE	$2,863,401	
Income Attributed to Vacancy and Concessions		
Goodwill Value	0%	$0
Value Loss due to Vacancy and Concessions		$0
LESS PERSONAL PROPERTY		
LESS TIEBACK		
LESS DEFERRED MAINTENANCE		
ADJUSTED MARKET VALUE		$2,863,401
COMMENTS:		

Chapter 13, Table 2

This analysis shows how even small differences in assumptions can cause a large difference in the final results. Compare the assumptions for the two cases. The differences in the individual assumptions are small. However, *small changes result in a 45 percent reduction in the final value!*

The critical issue in the income approach is understanding how to determine each of the elements (market rent, vacancy, expenses, etc.) from market data. The final conclusion for each of the assumptions used to prepare the income approach is subjective. For example, the best indication of the market rent for the subject property is the current rents being charged. However, there are often different rental rates being charged to different tenants at the subject property. The market vacancy is also a subjective issue. It may be higher or lower than the actual vacancy at the subject property. Again, actual other income at the subject property may be greater than or less than the market level of other income.

The same is true for each expense item. The analysis becomes more detailed when the operating expenses are analyzed individually, based on reviewing actual market expenses. Applying the income approach requires considerable market data and judgment regarding conclusions for each line item.

Other methods of performing the income approach include the gross income multiplier and a discounted cash flow analysis (DCF). Gross income multipliers are typically not used for property tax hearings for commercial properties. However, this method is sometimes used for moderately priced rent houses. This method involves multiplying the monthly gross income (before vacancy) for the subject property times a market-derived gross income multiplier. The gross income multiplier is derived from comparable sales by dividing the purchase price for the comparable sale by the monthly gross income at the time it sold. The gross rent multiplier is also used for commercial properties, except the analysis uses the annual rental rate instead of the monthly rental rate used for houses.

For example, assume a house is rented for $1,200 per month and the gross income multiplier for the submarket is 100. The market value of the house, assuming it is achieving a market level of rent, is $120,000 ($1,200 x 100). If the property were rented for $1100, the estimated market value using this technique would be $110,000 ($1,100 x 100).

A discounted cash flow analysis is more subjective than the direct capitalization analysis. Appraisal districts sometimes use the discounted cash flow analysis to calculate the present value of a property in a market with vacancy above the long-term stabilized level. It is typically not employed by property owners during property tax hearings.

The mechanics of performing the discounted cash flow analysis exceed the scope of our discussion of the income approach. Performing such analysis involves calculating the present value of all future cash flows from the property, including normal operations, capital improvements and selling the property.

In conclusion, the income approach offers an excellent opportunity to reduce property taxes for an income property. Performing the income approach requires a large quantity of data and an understanding of how the subject property contrasts with the market. However, the income approach is the primary approach considered at property tax hearings for income properties.

TEST OF REASONABLENESS

Consider the reasonableness of the results after performing the income approach. If you believe your property is probably worth $1 million and the value indicated by the income approach analysis is significantly above or below that level, you probably need to reconsider the individual elements. A moderately conservative value is appropriate for a property tax hearing. A ridiculously low value is not likely to generate satisfactory results.

The final step in considering the income approach for the property tax protest hearing is to compare the assessed value of the subject property with your market-value conclusion from an income approach analysis. If your income approach indicates a value less than the assessed value, it will probably be useful at the property tax protest hearing. If your income approach indicates a market value greater than the assessed value, it would not be prudent to use it at the property tax hearing.

Chapter 14: Cost Approach

The cost approach is not used at most property tax protest hearings in Texas. The sales comparison approach is typically used for houses, owner-occupied commercial properties, and raw land while the income approach is generally used for income-producing properties.

However, in certain specific cases, such as for relatively new properties (less than three years old), the cost approach may be useful. It is also useful for special use properties. Due to the difficulty of accurately estimating replacement cost and correctly calculating all types of depreciation, the cost approach is difficult to apply. Correctly calculating the market value when using the cost approach for a special use property is a detailed exercise requiring voluminous research in order to calculate depreciation correctly. Precisely estimating functional and external obsolescence is difficult and tedious.

REPLACEMENT COST VERSUS REPRODUCTION COST

Replacement cost is the current cost to build the functional equivalent of an existing building, using modern materials and construction methods. Reproduction cost is the cost to build an exact duplicate of a building, using identical materials and construction methods from the period when the building was constructed. Reproduction cost is typically higher than replacement cost since it often involves outdated or not easily available construction materials and construction methodology. Most appraisals are based on replacement costs.

Replacement cost can be estimated using cost handbooks such as Marshall & Swift or RSMeans. Contractors and developers are a good source of current construction costs. The actual construction cost for a recently built property is the best source of data regarding construction cost. There may be an exception if the construction costs were above what is typical or appropriate. In addition to the "hard costs," appraisers typically make allowances for soft costs and entrepreneurial profit. **Soft costs** include items such as property taxes during construction, architectural costs, engineering costs, appraisals, environmental studies, etc. **Entrepreneurial profit** can be defined as the amount of money necessary to induce a developer to organize the land, construction, debt, and equity financing necessary to complete a project. **Replacement cost is the sum of the actual construction costs, soft costs, the market value of land, and entrepreneurial profit.**

 PRACTICE TIP–Investors and tax consultants often omit soft costs and entrepreneurial profit when calculating replacement cost for property tax purposes.

Correctly calculating depreciation is one of the most technically difficult aspects of real estate appraisal. There are many forms of depreciation and detailed guidelines for their application. Appraisers often differ on the technically correct method of calculating depreciation. In practice, the appraiser would research and analyze market trends before calculating depreciation. The precise calculation of depreciation may vary from one market to another. Following is a summary of the major types of depreciation and a description of how they are applied.

Physical depreciation is based on wear and tear which occurs from the elements and normal use of a building. Physical depreciation is often divided into long-life and short-life components.

The **long-life components** have an economic life the same as the shell of the building. Examples of long-life components include foundations, wiring, plumbing, and the structure.

Short-life components have an economic life shorter than the economic life of the structure. These include roofs, paving, carpet, tile, HVAC, exterior paint, and window coverings.

There are several essential elements in calculating physical depreciation:

Effective age is "the age of property that is based on the amount of observed deterioration and obsolescence it has sustained, which may be different from its chronological age." *The Dictionary of Real Estate Appraisal,* 6th edition.

Economic life is "the period over which improvements to real property contribute to property value," *The Dictionary of Real Estate Appraisal,* 6th edition.

Sample Short-Life Depreciation Calculation

Short-life depreciation is calculated by multiplying the ratio of the effective age divided by economic life (effective age plus remaining economic life) of each component, times its replacement cost. For example, if the carpet in a building has an effective age of three years, an economic life of six years, and a cost of $1,000,

Depreciation = (3 years ÷ 6 years) x $1,000 = $500

Sample Long-Life Depreciation Calculation

The following is an example of calculating long-life depreciation. Suppose a building has an effective age of 5 years and a remaining economic life of 35 years, a total construction cost of $100,000, and short-life components totaling $10,000. Depreciation is:

Long-life Depreciation = 5 / (5+35) x ($100,000 — $10,000) = $11,250

The replacement cost of short-life items is subtracted from the total replacement cost before calculating long-life depreciation since depreciation for short-life items is calculated separately.

DEFERRED MAINTENANCE

Deferred maintenance is the result of not performing routine repairs or replacing short-life items timely. The cost to cure deferred maintenance should be deducted from the value derived in each of the three approaches to value (cost, income, and sales comparison).

Information on deferred maintenance can be helpful in property tax protest hearings. For the information to be effective, you should take photographs of deferred maintenance and obtain written bids from independent contractors. Take multiple copies of the bids and photographs to the hearing since the appraisal district staff or the ARB will require a copy for their file.

FUNCTIONAL OBSOLESCENCE

Functional obsolescence is the result of a design deficiency or spending too much on improvements. Routine functional obsolescence results from design flaws. Super adequacy is the result of spending more on improvements that do not generate value recognized by the market. Design deficiencies could include:

Multistory warehouse (most modern warehouses have only one story),

House without windows,

House with low ceiling height,

Large house with only one bedroom,

House without servant quarters in an area where quarters are typical,

Inferior grade construction materials in an executive home, construction of a Class C office building in an area where

Class A office buildings are prevalent,

Construction of a retail shopping center on a tertiary street,

Motel in a location that is difficult to find, and

Apartments built with too few amenities.

Super adequacy is a result of spending more for a building or component than the market is willing to compensate for in an arm's-length sale or lease transaction. Examples of super adequacy include building:

- A $500,000 home in an area where $100,000 homes are prevalent,

- A $20,000 marble fireplace in a $50,000 home,

- A high-rise office building with 20-foot ceilings on all floors in an area where 10-foot ceilings are prevalent,

- A warehouse with an 80-foot eave height in an area where a 28-foot eave height is typical,

- Apartments with too many amenities, and

- A four-star luxury hotel in a blue-collar area.

Functional deficiencies can be curable or incurable. An example of an incurable functional deficiency is a building with a seven-foot ceiling height in an area where eight-foot ceiling heights are typical. An example of a curable functional deficiency is a building built with a three-ton air conditioning system which needs a five-ton air conditioning system. A deficiency is curable if the cost to cure the deficiency is less than the incremental value generated by curing the deficiency. If a functional deficiency is curable, the depreciation adjustment is the cost to cure the problem. If a functional deficiency is not curable, the depreciation adjustment is the loss in value caused by the deficiency. This is often difficult, if not impossible, to calculate precisely. For example, how do you calculate the loss in value of a home with seven-foot ceilings in an area where eight-foot ceilings are typical?

If only one home in a subdivision of 500 homes has a seven-foot ceiling height while the balance has an eight-foot ceiling height, how much less would a purchaser pay? The most direct way to resolve this question is a sale of the subject property compared to sales of similar homes in the area. If the subject property has not sold recently, a comparison of similar properties with the same deficiency but located in other areas may be helpful, if such properties exist. However, locating this type of comparable sale is difficult and time-consuming.

For income properties, the loss in value can be estimated by estimating the annual rental loss due to the deficiency. The rental loss could be caused by a lower rental rate and/or higher vacancy. This amount can then be capitalized (divided by the capitalization rate) to calculate a depreciation adjustment for the functional deficiency.

Calculating functional depreciation for super adequate items or properties is even more difficult. If only one 5,000-square-foot home exists in an area where 1,000-square-foot homes are prevalent, the value is difficult to calculate. Adjustments for supera dequacy typically involve significant individual judgment, which renders the cost approach less reliable.

EXTERNAL OBSOLENSCENCE

External obsolescence results from sources outside a property. External obsolescence can be caused by a soft rental market or obnoxious or offensive surrounding properties. Examples of obnoxious or offensive surrounding properties could include a hog slaughtering plant, a topless bar adjacent to a Class A office building, and poorly maintained apartments in an area with million-dollar homes.

 PRACTICE TIP–To determine external obsolescence due to an undesirable neighbor for an income property, compare current market rent for similar properties without the undesirable neighbor to the rent at the subject property, and capitalize the difference.

The external obsolescence due to overbuilding is often calculated by comparing depreciated replacement cost rental rates to current market rental rates and capitalizing the

O'Connor Tax Reduction Experts 713.369.5958

difference. Calculation of external obsolescence for an income property with an obnoxious neighbor can be performed by estimating market rent without the neighbor versus actual current rent. The result is multiplied by the vacancy rate, assuming properties should achieve market occupancy. Total rent loss is divided by the capitalization rate to calculate external obsolescence.

Example:

Assume a 100,000-square-foot Class A office building is built next to a hog slaughtering facility. The market rent (without the hog slaughtering facility) would be $32 per square foot, but the average actual rent is only $16 per square foot. Both market and actual occupancy are 90 percent, and the market capitalization rate is 9 percent. The capitalization rate is not affected by the plant (to keep our example simple).

$16,000,000 = 100,000 x $16 x 90%÷9%

External obsolescence for owner-occupied properties can be calculated by comparing the sales price of properties near the obnoxious neighbor to sales prices for similar properties not influenced by the obnoxious neighbor. This can be difficult to calculate, depending on the availability of data. However, many homeowners are able to show that a home near objectionable commercial properties quickly loses value in comparison to homes buffered by other single-family homes.

210

For those desiring more information about the cost approach, *The Appraisal of Real Estate*, 14th edition, published by the Appraisal Institute contains a detailed description.

SUMMARY OF THE COST APPROACH

The first step is to estimate land value and to calculate total replacement costs, including construction costs, soft costs, and entrepreneurial effort. The second step is to deduct all forms of depreciation, including physical, functional, and external.

Physical depreciation is often divided into short-life and long-life depreciation. The total amount of all forms of depreciation is then deducted from the total replacement cost. Adding land value to the depreciated replacement cost results in the market value via the cost approach. A sample cost approach is summarized on the next page:

SAMPLE COST APPROACH

Replacement Cost (Construction Costs)	$100,000
Entrepreneurial Effort	10,000
Soft Costs	5,000
TOTAL REPLACEMENT COST	**$115,000**
LESS DEPRECIATION	
Physical	$20,000
Functional Deficiency	5,000
Superadequacy	-0-
External	5,000
TOTAL DEPRECIATION	**$30,000**
Replacement Cost Less Depreciation	$85,000
Plus Land Value	$20,000
VALUE VIA COST APPROACH	**$105,000**

Chapter 14, Table 1

PRACTICE TIP–The cost approach is seldom used at appraisal district hearings for houses, with the exception being new houses when the appraisal district's estimate of value is high. It is also used by appraisal districts to estimate the value of an owner-occupied commercial property. Most appraisal district hearings focus on either the sales comparison or income approaches. Appraisal districts prefer the cost approach for valuing business personal property. However, appraisal district depreciation schedules routinely overvalue personal property.

The thought of gathering the data and performing the calculations necessary for the cost approach may be intimidating. However, the cost approach is seldom used at property tax protest hearings except for new properties. If your property is relatively new (less than three years old), compare the construction costs with the appraisal district's estimated value of the improvements. The appraisal district will separately value the land and improvements for your property.

If the construction costs are less than the appraisal district's estimate, the cost approach is worth considering. The cost approach may also be worth considering if there are functional deficiencies or super adequate aspects of the property. The cost approach should also be considered when external obsolescence occurs. If apartments were built but the health of the apartment market subsequently declined, the market value of the apartments may be less than the total cost. Understanding these basic principles will prepare you for most property tax hearings without the necessity of becoming skilled in the technical nuances of precisely performing the cost approach.

 PRACTICE TIP–Rather than attempting to prepare the cost approach from scratch, ask the appraisal district for their cost analysis of your property. If they do not provide it upon request, just send an open records request. There is no information in the cost approach that would be confidential, based on Texas open records laws.

Chapter 15: Uniform And Equal

Texas allows for property tax appeals based on what is known as an unequal appraisal. It is also known as equity. The terms of evidence are an unequal appraisal analysis, or U & E. Texas has had a uniform and equal provision for many years, but until recently it has not been practical to protest on this basis. However, in 1997 the Texas legislature modified the Texas Property Tax Code to allow property owners a practical way to protest based on uniform and equal.

The basic concept of uniform and equal is that you should not be assessed for more taxes than your neighbor. For example, assume there are four corners at the intersection of two streets. Further, assume each of the four corners is worth $100,000. If three of the lots were assessed for $80,000 and one of the lots was assessed for $100,000, it would appear the owner of the lot assessed for $100,000 was being taxed excessively. Even though the lot is worth $100,000, the assessment for his neighbors with similar lots is 20 percent lower.

The dilemma with the pre-1997 Texas Tax Code was the amount of work necessary to prepare for a uniform and equal hearing. Most staff appraisers and appraisal review boards would not consider information regarding the assessment of other properties in the area during protest hearings. They wanted an independent fee appraisal of the subject property along with an appraisal of the assessment comparables for a large number of similar nearby properties. The cost of performing this analysis was often greater than the probable tax savings. Therefore, uniform and equal had not been used extensively in Texas, even though it has been technically available for many years, prior to the 1997 statute.

In 1997 the Texas legislature changed the Texas Property Tax Code to allow a uniform and equal protest based on "a reasonable number of comparable properties appropriately adjusted." Section 41.43, which is subtitled "Protest of Inequality of Appraisal," reads as follows:

In a protest authorized by Section **41.41(1) and (2)**, the appraisal district has the burden of establishing the value of the property by a preponderance of the evidence presented at the hearing. If the appraisal district fails to meet that standard, the protest shall be determined in favor of the property owner. **(Note – 41.41 (1) allows for protests if the appraised value exceeds market value and 41.41 (2) allows for protest if the property is unequally appraised.)**

A protest on the ground of unequal appraisal of property shall be determined in favor of the protesting party unless the appraisal district establishes that the appraisal ratio of the property is not greater than the median level of appraisal of:

- a reasonable and representative sample of other properties in the appraisal district;

- a sample of properties in the appraisal district consisting of a reasonable number of other properties similarly situated to, or of the same general kind or character as, the property subject to the protest;

or

-a reasonable number of comparable properties appropriately adjusted.

Appeals court decisions have ruled favorably on unequal appraisal analysis compiled using 7 comparables. In practice, some unequal appraisal analyses have as few as 1 comparable, a favorably assessed neighbor.

 PRACTICE TIP–Contrary to theory, in practice, 1 or 2 good assessment comparables is sometimes sufficient with a sympathetic appraiser or appraisal review board. Most appraisers typically interpret a reasonable number of comparable sales necessary to perform the sales comparison approach as, perhaps, 3 to 8. In some cases, appraisers use 2 to 3 sales to perform the sales comparison approach. In practice, most appraisal district unequal appraisal analysis includes 3 to 9 assessment comparables.

A bright line trend during the last twenty-one years (1997 to 2018) is that appraisal districts have a visceral dislike for unequal appraisal. It appears the basis is partially pride in their values, deep resentment at the implication they are not fairly valuing property and resentment of an approach to tax appeals that can usually support a reduction.

Proving it is still possible to be naïve at the age of 60, the author is dumbfounded at the practice of appraisal districts to shamelessly present unequal appraisal evidence that generates a predetermined value, namely the noticed value for the subject property. The more honest of the "predetermined values" is exactly the same as the subject property value.

The more deceitful generate an unequal appraisal analysis designed to generate a predetermined value but disguise their intent by inducing some type of rounding error or other minor error so the adjusted value for the comparables is very close, but may vary by up to 1 or 2%. Adjusting a comparable to within 1 or 2% of the subject property value makes it seem like good technical work. However, is it possible to adjust a warehouse built in 2010 (assessed for $100 PSF) to a warehouse built in 1910 (assessed for $15 PSF) and generate a value within 1 or 2% of the 1910 warehouse value?

Of course, there is no way to credibly adjust a warehouse built in 2010 to one built in 1910. However, examples like this occur daily in the unequal appraisal analysis we receive from appraisal districts. Such anecdotes simply illustrate the worthless nature of the unequal appraisal analysis prepared by appraisal districts.

Compounding the problem is that most appraisers will not consider unequal appraisal at the informal hearing or at the appraisal review board (ARB). The appraisal review boards are contemptuous of unequal appraisal evidence. In many cases, appraisal review board members either discard the evidence when it is handed to them or deliberately ignore the entire property owner evidence package.

Most ARB members take their service seriously and want to be independent. There are still structural impediments to an independent ARB:

- ARB members should elect a chairman.

- ARB members should be paid by the ARB and not the appraisal district.

The appraisal district used to select the ARB members. They are now selected by the administrative judge for the district courts in each county. However, he is too busy running his own court and handling administrative matters for other district courts to make the selection of ARB members a priority.

Most ARB members are serving for financial reasons. Even though the administrative judge has been appointing ARB members for about five years, there are extensive problems with ARB appointments.

Some central appraisal district staff have suggested that a reasonable number needs to be a statistically reasonable number, perhaps 100 or 500. Property tax attorney, James Popp, during his presentations at the 1998 and 1999 Texas A&M Ad Valorem Conferences proposed that a reasonable number is similar to the number of comparable sales an appraiser would use in a sales comparison approach.

The appropriate adjustments are somewhat subjective. James Popp further suggested that the adjustments should be performed in the same manner that they would be performed in the sales comparison approach for an appraisal. This suggests that adjustments be made for items such as age, building size, land-to-building ratio, and location. Real estate appraisers typically use a grid format to apply adjustments. A typical adjustment grid is shown in the following table:

SAMPLE ADJUSTMENT GRID

Location	Typical	Typical	Corner Lot	Typical	Typical	Typical
Assessed Value PSF Adjustment	$50	$41	$50	$45	$50	$42
Age		4	0	-3	-2	2
Size		6%	-3%	-6%	3%	0
Land Area		0	-10%	0	0	0
Condition		0	5%	0	-5%	0
Location		0	-5%	0	0	0
Total Adjustments		10%	-13%	-9%	-4%	2%
Adjusted PSF Assessed Value		$45.10	$43.50	$40.95	$48.00	$42.84

Median Assessed Value: $43.50

Subject Assessed Value: $150,000

Subject Assessed Value at Median: $130,500

(3,000 sf x $43.50 PSF)

Chapter 15, Table 1

Protests for uniform and equal are not being considered by all appraisal districts. Some appraisal districts have decided not to consider protests for uniform and equal at the informal hearings. Appraisal review boards at some appraisal districts declined to consider the information presented regarding uniform and equal. The future ability to protest using the uniform and equal provision of the Texas Tax Code will be resolved by the courts and legislature. During the interim, the provision will be utilized by some central appraisal districts in appraisal review boards and not by others.

221

Following are suggestions for protesting your property taxes until the future of uniform and equal is resolved:

Prepare a uniform and equal grid analysis as part of your hearing preparation.

Also, prepare a market value analysis if it supports a reduction.

Thoughtfully present your uniform and equal analysis at both the informal hearing and, if necessary, the appraisal review board hearing. Be prepared to be interrupted at either hearing, depending on the staff and the appraisal review board. Some may not consider this information.

Be prepared to cut short your presentation on uniform and equal, if it is not being considered. You may want to ask politely why they are not considering it, based on Section 41.43 of the Texas Property Tax Code. If your entire presentation and basis for a reduction in your property taxes is based on uniform and equal analysis, you may want to ask to speak to a supervisor. If the main portion of your protest is based on market value, pressing hard on the uniform and equal protest will likely hinder the market value portion of your protest.

If your main protest is based on uniform and equal, you may want to bring information on several comparable sales. Even if they aren't excellent comparable sales, they may provide the appraiser holding your hearing justification to reduce your assessed value.

Your property taxes may be reduced based on uniform and equal even if that is not the stated reason for the decrease. The informal appraiser holding the informal hearing may be sympathetic that your neighbors seem to be assessed for less even though the policy does not allow an adjustment based on equity. Having additional evidence (i.e., sales, deferred maintenance, errors on the record card) can help provide the staff appraiser a rationale for reducing your assessed value.

* * *

Chapter 16: Should You Hire An Appraiser?

Gathering data and performing the analysis for the market value and/or uniform and equal methodology is a time-consuming process. In order to save time, you may want to hire an independent appraiser to perform an appraisal of your property. There are pluses and minuses to this approach. An independent fee appraisal may receive more serious consideration at a property tax hearing than a handful of comparable sales presented by the property owner. Conversely, a carefully prepared and well-documented presentation demonstrates your concern that your property is over-assessed. While hiring an independent appraiser will reduce the time necessary to prepare for the protest hearing, the appraisal will increase the cost of the appeal process.

The first step to consider is the likely result of the independent appraisal. An appraisal with a market value greater than the assessed value of your property will not help reduce your property taxes. If your property is slightly undervalued and your objective is to obtain a modest additional reduction, an independent appraisal is probably not worthwhile.

If you believe the assessed value of your property exceeds the market, an independent appraisal is worth considering. Three important elements to consider are the following: 1) the potential property tax savings, 2) the cost of the appraisal, and 3) the time you will save. Calculate the potential tax savings by multiplying the estimated reduction in the assessed value times the total tax rate. For example, assume you have a property which is assessed for $320,000, actually worth $300,000 and has a three-percent tax rate. The potential tax savings is $600 ($20,000 x 3%).

Secondly, consider appraisal report options. Appraisers can perform either detailed or limited appraisals. A limited appraisal typically omits one or more of the approaches to value. A limited appraisal which considers only the sales comparison approach may be satisfactory for the appraisal of a home. A complete appraisal that includes all approaches is likely to yield meaningful and credible results. Discuss the appraisal options available with several appraisers to determine which format best fits your needs for the property tax hearing and with which appraiser you are most comfortable working.

The *third step* is to compare the potential property tax savings with the cost of the appraisal. You also need to consider the time saved by hiring the appraiser and your ability to gather data and perform appraisal analysis. Spending $200-$300 for an independent appraisal of a house would be worthwhile if it saves you $600 in taxes in the current year. In addition, tax savings obtained in the current year may be enjoyed for several years into the future. You will have to decide whether hiring an appraiser makes sense in your specific case. If you anticipate several hundred dollars in tax savings, contact several of appraisers and discuss this option.

Chapter 17: Subjective Nature Of The Appraisal Process

An appraisal is not a fact and an assessed value does not define market value. It is an *informed opinion* based on analyzing the subject property and market data (sales data, rent comparables, market vacancy, market expenses, capitalization rates, replacement costs, etc.). **The judgment of the appraiser is an integral part of the process.** Incorrect data or inaccurate judgment will result in an erroneous value. Market value is a topic on which reasonable people can disagree. This type of reasonable disagreement is the foundation of the property tax protest process and the property tax consulting profession.

Texas appraisal districts are generally staffed by highly skilled and professional individuals. However, they are charged with performing a large number of appraisals. As exemplified in the chart on page 51, the number of appraisals performed by individual staff appraisers at some of the largest Texas central appraisal districts is huge.

The crushing workload faced by the appraisers at the central appraisal districts generates an opportunity for property owners and tax agents. Property owners can spend significantly more time preparing for a property tax hearing than the appraisal district staff. In most cases, the appraisal district staff will start the informal hearing with a file on the subject property which they have not reviewed before the hearing. The staff appraiser performing the informal hearing typically will not ever have seen the subject property.

The property owner has a significant advantage since he or she can inspect the subject property, comparable sales, and assessment comparables and perform a careful, detailed analysis in preparation for the hearing. He can then decide which comparable sales to use. If appropriate, the property owner can also decide whether to present information regarding the income approach. In general, the property owner can perform a series of calculations and analyses and "cherry pick" which ones to present at the property protest hearing.

The Texas Tax Code requires central appraisal districts to reappraise every property every three years. Most large central appraisal districts appraise each property every two years. As stated earlier, most of these appraisals are performed using a mass appraisal methodology. Mass appraisal uses large databases, computer models, and statistical testing to estimate market value for each property. The accuracy of mass appraisal is dependent upon the data for the subject property, comparable sales data employed, and the computer model. Errors in any one of these three components can cause an incorrect value.

Appraisal districts spend significant effort developing accurate computer models. In most cases, the computer models are perceived to be reasonably accurate. The information on the subject property and comparable sales is often less accurate. The appraisal district is not able to visit each property each year. Discussions with the staff at several appraisal districts indicate that drive-by inspections are performed every 5 to 10 years. Appraisal districts gather large quantities of sales data for homes, commercial properties, and land. This data is obtained from taxpayers, data submitted in response to appraisal district questionnaires, and information from third parties. *While most of this information is probably accurate, information on any one property may be inaccurate.*

Real estate appraisal is not an exact science. It is a combination of data, technical analysis, and judgment. The inexact nature of real estate appraisal and the volume of properties appraised annually by central appraisal districts generate opportunities for property owners. *Over half of all protest hearings at large central appraisal districts in Texas result in a reduction in the assessed value and property taxes.*

Chapter 18: How To Prepare For A Protest Hearing

Preparing for a property tax protest hearing involves understanding the appraisal district's description of your property, gathering information related to the market value, performing a uniform and equal analysis, evaluating the evidence to present at the appraisal district, developing a negotiating position, and researching information the appraisal district is likely to use.

Gathering factual information about your property and documentation regarding assessment comparables and comparable sales will give you a sound basis to protest your property taxes. Some property owners appear for a property tax hearing without any evidence and rely on weak arguments such as vague statements that "crime is increasing in the area" or "my assessment went up more than property values rose in this area." Your chances of reducing your property taxes increase sharply when you properly prepare for the protest hearing.

Reviewing the central appraisal district's record card for your property is an excellent way to start the preparation process. The central appraisal district has record cards with more than 100 fields of data for thousands or even millions of properties. It is highly unlikely that all of this information is correct. You can obtain a copy of the record card for your property at your central appraisal district; there may be a small charge for this information. The staff at your central appraisal district can answer questions regarding the content and format of the record card.

After receiving the record card and asking questions regarding the layout and format, verify the accuracy of the information and document errors in the record card with a plat or with photos. If there are significant issues which overstate the quality or quantity of improvements of your property, you may want to have the appraisal district staff inspect your property. The staff at some appraisal districts is reluctant to accept assertions by property owners without verification.

Documentation of deferred maintenance is an excellent way to reduce your property taxes. Take photographs of any significant deferred maintenance items. Photographs of interior settling, cracks in exterior walls, water damage, rotten wood, peeling paint, and other similar types of deferred maintenance should be helpful in reducing your assessed value. However, taking 20 photographs of hairline cracks in your driveway or sidewalk will not be helpful in most cases. You may want to include one photograph showing the overall property if it will be helpful during the protest.

SALE OF THE SUBJECT

If your property was purchased recently, compare the purchase price to the assessed value. If the purchase price is less than the assessed value, information regarding the purchase price will be helpful in reducing your property taxes. If your property was purchased for more than the assessed value, presenting information on the purchase price will likely only increase the assessed value in future years. If your purchase price was more than your assessed value, your only possible route of protest is uniform and equal. Appraisal districts and appraisal review boards are not sympathetic to discussions regarding why you overpaid for the property. They have heard many explanations of why people overpaid and rarely reduce the assessed value in these cases.

DOCUMENT DEFERRED MAINTENANCE

Compiling bids to repair deferred maintenance is an effective method of reducing your assessed value. Most appraisal districts will not make adjustments for deferred maintenance without some documentation of the cost to remedy the problem. However, some will adjust the condition factor a level or two based on photographs.

DECIDE YOUR APPROACH TO VALUE

A central focus of the protest hearing process is to perform the relevant appraisal analysis. See Chapter 10 (page 135) regarding which approach to value should be performed for your property.

In summary, the appraisal district will focus on the following types of evidence:

Sales comparison approach—used primarily for houses, land, and owner-occupied commercial buildings

Income approach—used primarily for income properties

Cost approach—used primarily for projects which are under construction or up to two or three years old

If you are protesting an income property, most appraisal districts will be reluctant to adjust the assessed value until they review and consider the year-end profit and loss statement for the previous year and the rent roll. Very few appraisal districts will consider a uniform and equal analysis without reviewing the actual income information.

A uniform and equal analysis is an important element of preparing for the protest hearing although not all appraisal districts and appraisal review boards will use the information. However, you won't know if they will use the information until you appear for the hearing. The hearing process can be somewhat arbitrary, depending on the staff appraiser or appraisal review panel hearing your protest. One staff appraiser may consider your uniform and equal analysis while another may not. Even if the policy at the appraisal district is not to accept a uniform and equal analysis, the staff appraiser may reduce your assessed value if he is sympathetic to an inequitable situation.

PRACTICE TIP–*You need to have five copies of all evidence if you proceed to the appraisal review board.* Appraisal review boards can become testy and unfavorable if you do not provide copies. Call the central appraisal district to confirm how many copies to bring to the informal hearing.

DETERMINE YOUR NEGOTIATING POSITION

Effective negotiation requires an opening position and a fallback position. In most negotiations, you are unlikely to achieve the initial request in your opening position. Therefore, your opening position at the informal hearing should be a lower assessed value than you expect to achieve. The opening position is also referred to as the target value.

Your fallback position (or ARB value) should be the highest assessed value you will accept without going to the appraisal review board hearing. This is an important decision since you can't file a judicial appeal if you agree to a value at the informal hearing.

You may also want to consider presenting information in stages. For example, you could present most of your information initially but hold back some information until later in the process.

 PRACTICE TIP – For example, negotiate a value for your property based on the sales data. After agreeing on that value, request a further reduction based on adjusting the condition factor. Photos could support a reduction in the condition.

UNDERSTAND YOUR OPPONENT AND HIS POSITION

You should research for information that the appraisal district staff and appraisal review board are likely to consider during the hearing. This may include information on comparable sales and assessment comparables and their income model if your property is an income property. *You can obtain a copy of all the information the central appraisal district will consider at your property tax hearing by requesting it when you file your protest.* There may be a charge to obtain this information although the practice in many counties is not to charge individual taxpayers. Section 41.461, "Notice of Certain Matters Before Hearing," allows property owners or their agent to obtain information to be used by the central appraisal district before the hearing. This section is as follows:

Sec. 41.461. Notice of Certain Matters Before Hearing

At least 14 days before a hearing on a protest, the chief appraiser shall:

deliver a copy of the pamphlet prepared by the comptroller under Section 5.06(a) to the property owner initiating the protest if the owner is representing himself, or to an agent representing the owner if requested by the agent;

inform the property owner that the owner or the agent of the owner may inspect and may obtain a copy of the data, schedules, formulas, and all other information the chief appraiser plans to introduce at the hearing to establish any matter at issue;

and

deliver a copy of the hearing procedures established by the appraisal review board under Section 41.66 to the property owner.

The charge for copies provided to an owner or agent under this section may not exceed the charge for copies of public information as provided under Subchapter F, Chapter 552, Government Code, except:

the total charge for copies provided in connection with a protest of the appraisal of residential prop-city may not exceed $15 for each residence;

and

the total charge for copies provided in connection with a protest of the appraisal of a single unit of property subject to appraisal, other than residential property, may not exceed $25.

PRACTICE TIP – If the appraisal district tries to charge you $15 or $25 for a few sheets of paper, just snap an image of each page with your phone.

In summary, the steps necessary to prepare for a protest hearing include:

Reviewing the appraisal district's information regarding your property as found on its record card to determine its validity.

Gathering information related to the market value of your

property using the sales comparison, income, or cost approach.

Performing a uniform and equal analysis.

Evaluating the evidence to present to the district including information about deferred maintenance, errors in the district's information, and pertinent information about the subject property which may affect value.

Deciding on a negotiating position—both an initial and a fallback position.

Researching for information the appraisal district is likely to use by requesting this information prior to the hearing.

Completing these steps will prepare you for your property tax protest hearing. If your property is over assessed, this preparation should allow you to reduce your property tax assessed value at the hearing.

Chapter 19: How To Get The Appraisal District To Roll Out The Red Carpet For You!

There are two good means to get the red carpet treatment: 1) send a letter to the appraisal district's Taxpayer Liaison Officer or 2) present to the appraisal district's board of directors. These are both excellent options to resolve problems that were difficult to resolve through normal means.

Consider the following circumstances:

> - A homeowner has a difficult time getting a homestead exemption due to miscommunications with appraisal district staff.
> - The grade of your house (quality of construction and level of finish; starter home versus luxury home) is wrong.
> - The condition is not correct.
> - The land area is wrong.
> - The ownership is wrong.
> - The size of the house is wrong.
> - The exemption for adjacent lot is not granted. (If your residence is adjacent to a lot you own, include the lot in your "homestead" for property tax purposes).

Typically these errors are not committed to be punitive. Either the district has bad information or the process does not allow them to fix the issue.

While the Tax Code applies to all counties in Texas, each appraisal district is akin to a village in the middle ages in England. There is a ruler and whatever he says goes. The only real remedy if you can't get the appraisal district to comply with the Tax Code is to file a lawsuit in district court. In most cases, the appraisal district will comply. However, you will incur substantial expense to get the appraisal district to just follow the law. There is a better way.

 PRACTICE TIP – this one works best.

Option One

Politely, respectfully, succinctly and accurately describe the problem to the board of directors. In most cases, the chief appraiser or a member of appraisal district management will immediately comment. Typically, they will meet immediately to get your contact data. In some cases, they will take you to the person who can resolve the problem.

The chief appraiser serves "at the pleasure" of the board of directors of the appraisal district. If a taxpayer has been mistreated, the chief appraiser wants to take care of him

properly in most cases, and particularly, when he is in front
of the board of directors.

Here is a recent example. In the fall of 2017, I received a call
from a friend. He had purchased a house for $700,000 and it
was valued by HCAD for $1,000,000. HCAD has a policy of
not changing the market value more than $100,000 at the
informal hearing (with very, very, very, very few exceptions).
So the account had an appraisal review board hearing. The
impartial appraisal review board, (paid by the appraisal
district , logging their time with the appraisal district, having
their parking supervised by the appraisal district, and having
to get permission from the appraisal district to leave for
lunch), concluded on a value of perhaps $950,000. (Note:
these numbers are demonstrative but not actual.)

My friend uses us regularly for tax appeals but he thought it
would be a lay down (as it should have been). This was an
arm's-length sale that had been on the market for over 12
months. He was SHOCKED at the ARB decision.

He had called me to engage my firm, O'Connor, to
coordinate a lawsuit in district court or to file for binding
arbitration. My counsel was to recommend that he politely
describe to the HCAD board of directors his purchase of the
property, the extended marketing period, and the unfortunate
ARB result.

The client was not comfortable with public speaking so we discussed the options several times. The benefits of presenting to the board of directors include: 1) faster resolution 2) no fees from our firm 3) there is still time to coordinate a lawsuit or binding arbitration, and 4) no cost to client except an hour or two of his time. The potential tax savings were about $7,000; not bad for two hours work.

The client decided to present to the board of directors. An appraisal district employee contacted him immediately after his presentation (less than 30 seconds). The next day he received a call from a senior appraiser agreeing to reduce the 2017 value to $700,000, the purchase price. This was a great resolution at low cost. It had the added benefit of pointing out problems at the appraisal district. The more feedback citizens provide the appraisal district with, the better they can serve all property owners.

Option Two

The second alternative is to send a letter to the Taxpayer Liaison Officer (TLO). The TLO is required for counties with a population of at least 125,000. The TLO is responsible for investigating reports from property owners and reporting to the appraisal district board of directors at the next meeting, or until the issue is resolved.

Legitimate issues are typically resolved by the TLO.

Chapter 20: Attending The Protest Hearing

Congratulations! You are now prepared to attend the protest hearing. You have analyzed both the market value and the assessed value for your property. After studying the central appraisal district's records for your property, you understand mistakes in its records, and you understand which of your neighbors' properties are assessed for less than yours, making your assessment inequitable. After reviewing this information, you have developed both a target value (opening negotiating position) and an ARB value (the highest value which you will accept before going to the appraisal review board hearing).

HELPFUL HINTS FOR THE HEARING

Arrive early before the hearing to ensure you are on time. At some appraisal districts, such as the Dallas Central Appraisal District, you may need to show up a day or two ahead of time or perhaps one or two hours early to perform the informal hearing before the scheduled time. At these appraisal districts, the scheduled time is for the appraisal review board hearing rather than the informal hearing. If you want to attend an informal hearing—and it is usually worthwhile to attend—plan to do so before your scheduled time. You may not want to attend the informal hearing if a recent sales price exceeds the assessed value of your property or if there is information you do not wish to present at the informal hearing which is likely to be requested (i.e., financial statements for income property). *Call the appraisal district to find out whether the scheduled time is for the informal hearing or the appraisal review board hearing and plan accordingly.*

Spend a few minutes developing a rapport with the district's informal appraiser before discussing the technical aspects of your case. In general, time is on your side. Spend as much time as the appraiser wants in discussing general topics or topics of mutual interest. While the appraiser's decision may not be influenced because you have developed some limited level of rapport, he is more likely to show flexibility to someone he enjoys working with compared to someone who is belligerent or rude.

PRACTICE TIP — "Seek first to understand, then to be understood" -Stephen Covey. Understanding the hearing from the appraiser's perspective is helpful.

The appraisal districts typically allow about 15 minutes for each informal hearing. Present the technical elements of your case in a calm and logical manner. Present supporting details without belaboring the points. Try to perceive your presentation from the staff appraiser's perspective. The staff appraiser attending the informal hearing is likely a trained appraiser and should be able to digest quickly the technical content you are presenting.

WHAT NOT TO DO

Do not attack the appraiser who meets with you at the informal hearing. This can only hurt your chance of achieving a reduction. Would you be more likely to grant an adjustment to a cordial, friendly person logically presenting information or an obnoxious person complaining that his taxes are too high because you are overpaid and the government wastes his money?

Do not complain about high taxes. The informal appraiser's task is to meet with you and consider information as to why the market value is less than the assessed value and perhaps why the home is not equitably assessed. The staff appraiser does not set state-wide tax policy. Nor does he set the tax rates for any taxing entity or control the effectiveness of expenditures by tax entities. The appraiser hears many complaints about high taxation which he is powerless to address. One exception where politely grumbling about high taxes may work is if you are an elderly homeowner who wants to express a lack of ability to pay your taxes and still buy food and other basic essentials. In summary:

DO be polite and friendly.

DO present factual information in a logical order.

DO NOT be insulting or belligerent.

DO NOT complain about high taxes which the appraiser cannot control.

WORKING EFFECTIVELY WITH A STAFF APPRAISER TO ACHIEVE A MUTUALLY BENEFICIAL RESULT

After carefully stating your technical presentation, listen attentively to the appraiser's response or questions. Some of his questions could be an attempt to develop information which would be helpful in reducing the assessed value for your property. *It is important to maintain a cooperative dialogue during the hearing.* The appraiser will likely present information regarding the central appraisal district's assessed value and the data supporting it. Probe and ask questions about their information, such as the condition of the property, the source of the sales information, how it was verified, etc. You may also want to ask about the date the central appraisal district last visited the property. If before the hearing you researched the sales the central appraisal district is likely to use or requested that they present this information to you, you had a chance to review and verify this information with buyers and sellers or with real estate agents. If some of the information is inaccurate, discuss this with the appraiser as a reason to place more emphasis on your data and less on some of the appraisal district's data.

MOTIVATIONS OF THE PROPERTY OWNER AND CENTRAL DISTRICT APPRAISER

The *property owner's objective is* primarily to reduce property taxes. In some cases, correcting the property record card is important to correct the problem permanently. For example, if the central appraisal district indicates that the house has 2,000 square feet while it has only 1,700 square feet, correcting this error will likely reduce the assessed value in future years.

Equitable assessment is a critical and emotionally charged issue for some property owners. It may be more important to them to be assessed equitably compared to their neighbors than to reduce their property taxes. The author has heard literally hundreds of property owners share their distress that their neighbors are assessed for less even though those neighbors' houses are nicer. In many cases, this emotional concern overrides the economics.

The *central appraisal district appraiser's objective* is to resolve the hearing in a timely manner while minimizing the reduction in the assessed value. ("Value Loss" is the reduction in value due to informal and formal hearings.) There will be exceptions if the property is grossly overvalued. However, the staff appraisers are evaluated either formally or informally based on how many hearings they perform and the amount of the reductions granted at the hearings. Hence, a quick hearing with a modest reduction can be an attractive outcome for the staff appraiser, even if the subject property is already modestly under-assessed.

If your property is already slightly under assessed, focus on sales which support a lower value or assessment comparables which support a lower value.

Harris County Appraisal District had 382,555 protests in 2016. Large central appraisal districts conduct over 50,000 hearings per year. Since most appraisal districts conduct hearings during only two or three months of the year and since they conduct a large number of hearings where both sides typically compromise there is pressure to conclude each hearing quickly.

Central appraisal districts are receptive to giving small reductions to already under-assessed properties for several reasons. Granting small decreases in value increases the pace at which hearings occur. It also decreases the number of appraisal review board hearings. Appraisal review board hearings are more expensive to conduct than informal hearings because of the larger number of people which are required. Granting modest reductions also generates some goodwill with property owners. The appraisal district is a quasi-political entity. Continued employment of the senior staff is dependent upon the goodwill of the tax entities. Antagonizing large numbers of property owners could be detrimental to the continued employment of appraisal district personnel.

THE NEGOTIATION PROCESS

The informal appraiser will give you one of three offers after meeting for 5 to 20 minutes and discussing the information presented:

He may offer to reduce the assessed value,

He may indicate that he will not make any change,

or

He may suggest that he will recommend an increase at the ARB level if you do not agree to the value initially set for your property

It is unusual for an informal appraiser to recommend an increase, but if the informal appraiser does recommend one, you should seriously consider your options as discussed below.

IF THE APPRAISER OFFERS A REDUCTION

Depending on the appraiser, the first offer may or may not

be the best offer. If the offer is attractive, you may wish simply to accept it and conclude the hearing. However, in most cases, it would be worthwhile to continue the negotiation.

The next step will likely be to discuss the best information you have presented to support your position. Relax, go slowly, smile and present the information without being argumentative or abusive. Remember that time is on your side: the appraiser is expected to perform three or four hearings per hour. Act as though you have all day to discuss this and as though it is the most important project you have for the day.

Since your initial request was not your bottom line number, make a counteroffer after discussing why you think the assessed value should be lower. (There may be rare cases such as the sale of a subject property where the initial position is the only acceptable conclusion. However, even if the subject property sold recently, the uniform and equal analysis is likely to indicate that a lower assessed value is appropriate.) The objective of your counteroffer is to convey flexibility along with an ardent desire to resolve the hearing and reduce your property taxes.

The next response from the appraiser is probably his best offer or very close to it. Except for large commercial projects, appraisers have to resolve hearings quickly. Hence, they do not have time to spend 30 minutes to an hour going through an 8- or 10-step process of negotiation on each home or small commercial property. Consider the appraiser's offer and remain friendly, cooperative, and relaxed and appear to be unconcerned about the time even if you are desperate to leave as quickly as possible.

When the appraiser gives you his best offer, you have two choices: accept the offer or go to the appraisal review board. Evaluate the appraiser's offer versus what you might be able to accomplish at the appraisal review board. If you believe an additional tax savings can be accomplished by proceeding to the appraisal review board and spending an extra 30 minutes to two hours of time in the hearing process, it is probably worthwhile to proceed to the appraisal review board hearing. However, if the appraiser is offering to adjust the assessed value to a level which is similar to or perhaps less than what you believe an impartial panel of three citizens may determine, accept the offer and the property tax protest is resolved for the current year.

If you decide not to accept the appraiser's final offer, you will need to go to the appraisal review board hearing. *Before concluding the informal hearing, ask the appraiser to recommend his offer to the appraisal review board.* This increases the chance that they will agree to that number or a lower number. The appraisal review board is not bound to the value which is offered by the appraiser. They may determine a value which is the same as, which is higher, or which is lower than the value offered by the informal appraiser. In rare cases, the appraisal review board will determine a value higher than the value initially assessed by the central appraisal district.

IF THE STAFF APPRAISER DOESN'T OFFER TO REDUCE YOUR ASSESSED VALUE

If the staff appraiser does not agree to a reduction, probe and continue the negotiation process. You may wish to ask the appraiser to discuss his data and analysis in more detail. If there are flaws in the data or analysis, tactfully discuss them. If you are presenting information regarding an equity analysis or uniform and equal concept which the informal appraiser has not considered, you may ask to speak to his supervisor regarding why they would not consider a uniform and equal presentation. It may be more desirable to grant a reduction than to locate and discuss the hearing with the supervisor.

If the appraiser still will not agree to a reduction in your assessed value after again reviewing both his information and your information, ask what he will recommend to the ARB. In some cases, the staff appraiser is willing to recommend a reduction to the ARB that he is not willing to agree to informally. Recommending a reduction to the ARB takes the pressure off the informal appraiser. The reduction will be attributed to the appraisal review board and not to the informal appraiser.

If the informal appraiser is willing to recommend a reduction to the ARB, it is likely worthwhile spending the additional time to attend the ARB hearing. If the informal appraiser is not willing to recommend a reduction to the ARB, review both your information and the appraisal district's information presented at the informal hearing and decide whether it is likely that a three-member citizen panel will agree to a reduction based upon the available information. Also, consider the probable tax savings if a reduction is granted and consider whether the tax savings merits the time required.

IF THE APPRAISER WILL NOT DECREASE THE VALUE AND STATES THAT HE WILL RECOMMEND AN INCREASE TO THE ARB

If the staff appraiser indicates he will recommend an increase if you continue the hearing at the ARB level, consider this to be a serious threat. Staff appraisers seldom recommend increases. For the staff appraiser to recommend an increase to the ARB, it typically means he feels that the property is grossly under assessed and the protest is frivolous or abusive.

If the reason the staff appraiser is recommending an increase is not clear, probe to understand his reasoning. It is possible there was a misunderstanding regarding the subject property or the analysis you presented. Assuming there has not been a misunderstanding, carefully weigh the potential benefits of attending the ARB hearing versus the potential increase in property taxes if the ARB accepts the staff appraiser's recommended value. The ARB typically will not grant an increase, but there are a limited number of cases where they do increase the initial assessed value.

The staff appraiser must allow you to accept the noticed value (initial assessed value) if he is planning to recommend an increase to the ARB. (You cannot be compelled to attend the ARB hearing.) The value agreed to at the informal hearing may not be appealed further. However, the value decided upon at the ARB level may be appealed in district court.

PRESENENTING YOUR CASE TO THE ARB

If you do not accept the value offered at the informal hearing, the next step is to attend the appraisal review board hearing. The complete appraisal review board may have as many as 180 members in large counties. However, the ARB hearing for your protest will be a three-member panel. The three-member panel typically is rotated and the members are often assigned randomly so they do not work together as a team on a daily basis. The ARB panel members have a variety of backgrounds. Most do not have an extensive real estate background and are not full-time appraisers. However, they do receive a one-day class on real estate appraisal, Texas property tax law, and related issues. Counties with the largest numbers of appraisal review board members include:

County	Members
Harris	190
Dallas	95
Tarrant	85
Bexar	50
Fort Bend	35
El Paso	30

THE PLAYERS

In addition to the three-member ARB panel, a CAD appraiser will attend the ARB hearing along with the property owner or his agent. In some appraisal districts, a clerk handles paperwork and tapes the hearing. The appraisal district appraiser attending the hearing may or may not be the same appraiser who performed the informal hearing. In large counties, the appraiser at the ARB hearing is typically different from the appraiser who attended the informal hearing. One exception is with the largest commercial properties; the appraiser is likely to be the same person at both the informal and ARB hearings.

HELPFUL HINTS FOR THE ARB HEARING

You may have to wait 15 minutes to two hours between the informal hearing and the ARB hearing. If so, don't express your frustration to the ARB members, clerk, or staff appraiser. They did not intentionally cause you to wait and will likely react if you start the hearing by attacking them. *The appraisal review board hearing is not the time or place to express personal dissatisfaction with the high level of property taxes, the limited services you receive for them, or crime in the area.* The ARB panel members do not control the level of property taxes or the system for handling property taxes in Texas. Neither are they involved in the services you receive for the property taxes paid. While crime in the area may generally contribute or affect the value of your property, it similarly affects the value of comparable sales or rental income for the property which is implicit in the analysis presented by the property owner and the appraisal district.

Have five copies of all data and presentation material including pictures to make available to the ARB members and staff appraiser. This will increase the chance of effectively communicating your position during the limited time you have their attention. You can focus your presentation on either:

why the assessed value is higher than the market value

and/or

why your property is over assessed based on uniform and equal.

ARB Procedures

Most ARB hearings are organized as follows:

> ➢ ARB members affirm they haven't discussed the case before the hearing began.

> ➢ Property owner/agent affirms information presented is accurate.

> ➢ The clerk or an ARB member reads a description of the property which is then affirmed by the property owner.

> ➢ The property owner and central appraisal district appraiser present information and discuss the flaws and weaknesses in the other's argument. They may also ask questions of each other to clarify data or analysis.

> ➢ ARB members ask questions of the property owner/agent and the central appraisal district appraiser.

> ➢ ARB renders its decision which is typically non-negotiable.

It is unlikely the ARB will change its decision after it is announced. If its decision is acceptable, no further action is needed for the current tax year. You should review protesting the assessed value the subsequent year. If you are not satisfied with the ARB decision, your sole option is to appeal the result to the state district court by filing a lawsuit.

O'Connor Tax Reduction Experts 713.369.5958

This option is discussed in detail in the next chapter.

Chapter 21: Should You Appeal The Arb Decision? Factors To Weigh

There are a variety of factors indicating whether or not it makes sense to coordinate a judicial appeal (lawsuit in district court) or binding arbitration. The most important factor in this evaluation is the amount of dollar reduction possible, which is related to the value of the property. It is not financially feasible to pursue appeals beyond the appraisal review board unless the potential tax reduction exceeds a certain level. However, since the level of reduction possible is closely correlated to the taxable value of the house, it is not perceived to be financially feasible to pursue either a judicial appeal or binding arbitration for most typical houses which are valued at $200,000 to $350,000, depending on the location in Texas. The exception is houses valued substantially over market for any value. Our firm would gladly pursue binding arbitration for a house worth $40,000 and valued at $60,000.

Due to the perceived high cost of appealing the ARB decision in state district court, few judicial appeals are filed relative to the number of accounts and property tax protests. The following is a summary of the number of accounts, property tax protests, and judicial appeals or lawsuits filed in major counties in Texas in 1998 and in 2016:

PROPERTY TAX PROTESTS &

APPEALS IN TEXAS COUNTIES IN 1998

County	# of Accounts	# of Real Estate Protests	# of Lawsuits Filed
Harris	1,509,556	80,148	304
Dallas	1,067,219	51,556	291
Tarrant	545,931	38,340	149
Bexar	592,151	32,721	94
Travis	392,217	36,832	143
Hidalgo	284,278	8,013	13
Gregg	233,259	2,786	3
Montgomery	201,665	2,654	5

PROPERTY TAX PROTESTS &

APPEALS IN TEXAS COUNTIES IN 2016

County	# of Accounts	# of Real Estate Protests	# of Lawsuits Filed	# of Arbitrations Filed
Harris	1,623,452	382,55	4,492	7,667
Dallas	828,387	117,271	1,413	218
Tarrant	1,253,623	205,132	728	472
Bexar	671,217	95,721	1,177	504
Travis	423,981	115,733	716	204
El Paso	412,608	19,982	484	42
Denton	398,276	63,437	268	50
Collin	373,754	52,506	204	337
Fort Bend	339,581	72,083	117	334

The data for both charts came from the Texas Comptroller.

Chapter 21, Table 1

Consider the potential tax savings versus the cost and time involved in a judicial appeal when deciding whether or not to appeal the ARB decision. The primary costs involved in pursuing a judicial appeal include legal expenses, expert witness fees, and the time the property owner or his representative will spend during the appeal. The legal expenses will depend upon the legal counsel hired and the type of property. Since this is a specialized area, you should hire an attorney who specializes or spends a considerable portion of his time in property tax litigation. Active property tax litigators can give you an estimate of the costs after a brief discussion.

Expert witness fees typically involve real estate appraisers except in business personal property cases. The appraisal fees can be broken into two components: the cost to prepare an opinion of value, and the additional time spent in depositions, trial preparation, and trial. Most cases can be resolved without the appraiser spending time on depositions, trial preparation, or trial.

When engaging an appraiser, you may also wish to discuss the type of report necessary with both the appraiser and the attorney. In many cases, preparing a *shorter appraisal report* (letter appraisal) may dramatically reduce the cost and may provide data for the appraisal district and its attorneys to understand the basis of the property owner's argument. In other cases, it may not be necessary for the appraiser to prepare a written report after he develops an opinion of value.

Most property tax lawsuits are resolved through settlement negotiations instead of a trial. Less than one percent of lawsuits over market value for property taxes in Texas go to trial, according to personal observation and discussions with property tax attorneys. The settlement typically involves some reduction of the assessed value in property taxes. However, in some cases, lawsuits are not suitable for a variety of reasons. These can include a reluctance to invest in legal fees and expert witness costs, a reluctance to attend depositions, or a reluctance to comply with discovery requests and an exposure to higher taxes at trial.

SHOULD YOU FILE A JUDICIAL APPEAL?

BINDING ARBITRATION

Your decision regarding filing a judicial appeal should be made after considering the potential tax savings, costs, and time required. Sensitivity analysis is an appropriate technique for determining whether the judicial appeal will be fruitful. Review the net tax savings after legal and other costs for a variety of settlement levels to determine if a judicial appeal is financially attractive. Due to the volume of litigation in state district courts, cases are typically settled from 9 to 30 months after they are filed. The settlement may involve tax savings for two years, which may double the tax savings involved. Also, consider the potential long-term benefits of a reduction in the assessed value. Although a reduction may not be maintained beyond the tax years involved in the settlement, in many cases the settlement assessed value is not increased

O'Connor Tax Reduction Experts 713.369.5958

during the next year or two. Hence, the tax savings may extend over three to four years instead of one or two years. In addition, settlements or agreed assessed values for the current year are used as an anchor or base value for settlements in future years. The appraisal district is more receptive to reducing the assessed value to a base level established through administrative hearings or litigation once it is established.

Analyze the target value you can support through market data or assessment comparables in reviewing your judicial appeal. Depending upon the strength and accuracy of your analysis, you may or may not achieve a settlement at the target value. If a settlement midway between the target value and the ARB value justifies the expenditure of money and time, your judicial appeal merits serious consideration.

The appraisal review board will send you or your agent a notice of the assessed value established by the appraisal review board after the ARB hearing. This notice is typically sent two to four weeks after the hearing. The value established at the hearing is actually a proposed settlement which has to be ratified by the full ARB. The ARB panel that hears your account is typically composed of three members while in some counties the full appraisal review board consists of as many as 180 members. The full ARB routinely ratifies the decisions of the three-member ARB panels. Only in rare cases does it reject the recommendation and schedule a new hearing. *You have 60 days after you or your agent receives official notice of the ARB value to file a judicial appeal.* Since this notice is sent by registered or certified mail, return receipt requested, both the agent or property owner and the appraisal district are aware of exactly when the ARB notice was received.

You may want to consult an attorney and tax consultant in determining whether to file a judicial appeal. The attorney can estimate the legal expenses, the time frame to conclude a judicial appeal, the appraisal district's likely tactics, and the time required. The attorney may also be able to help estimate some of the other costs, such as the expert witness fees for the real estate appraiser. The attorney should know the appraisal district's approach to resolving litigation.

The tax consultant should provide guidance regarding the appraisal district's willingness to settle lawsuits versus trying them, which methodology and approaches (market value versus uniform and equal) the appraisal district will consider in a settlement, and how litigation may affect the value in future administrative hearings.

Consult an attorney for advice regarding whether to file a judicial appeal. This book is not intended to provide or be a substitute for legal counsel.

Chapter 22: Should You Hire A Property Tax Consultant?

Preparing for and presenting a property tax protest is a technical, tedious, and time-consuming process which requires significant data. However, tens of thousands of Texas property owners file their own protests and then prepare and present their own protest, annually. *You can effectively handle your own tax appeal if you spend the time to understand the process, gather the necessary information and prepare an appropriate analysis for the protest hearing.*

The primary issues to review are whether you are comfortable engaging in an adversarial process, whether it is the best use of your time, and whether you can generate results equal to what a tax consultant can accomplish. Some property owners are not inclined to undertake an oral presentation at the protest hearing, especially if they believe the other side is more knowledgeable and more familiar with the process. For others, the annual potential savings may not merit the time required. It probably takes an average homeowner 4 to 10 hours to prepare for and present a property protest through the ARB as detailed in previous chapters.

A related issue is whether you want to review data and protest annually. A skilled and organized property tax consultant (i.e., agent) is able to research information on your property and comparable sales efficiently, perform a comparable assessment analysis, and attend a property tax hearing on an annual basis. Much of this work can be done using computer databases. A single tax consultant, with appropriate administrative and technical support, can perform effectively 2,000 property tax protests annually.

 PRACTICE TIP – Ensuring that your property taxes are handled annually is one of the primary benefits of hiring a tax consultant. Despite the best of intentions, few property owners will both file a protest and attend the hearings. That's ALL we do during the summer, day after day until the end of the fall. We completed over 160,000 protest hearings in 2017. However, to be clear, the author strongly believes that most homeowners can handle their property tax protest. His concern is that they will not protest annually. Protesting annually is essential for homeowners to get the deep discounts that commercial property owners receive. Our firm has helped thousands of clients annually (for 5+ years) receive home valuations at 70% of market value or less.

The agent's services usually include filing the protest, researching sales, performing an income analysis (if appropriate), and performing a uniform and equal analysis. In years when this information supports a reduction, the agent will request the reduction in your assessed value at the hearing. The consultant should also obtain the appraisal district's evidence if it is one of the appraisal districts that follow the law. If the data does not support a reduction, the agent will agree to the notice value at the hearing. Due to the limited time between when assessed values are announced and when the protest is due, many agents protest all accounts to ensure that all over-assessed accounts are protested. Protesting all accounts is referred to as a "blanket protest."

If your agent is billing based upon only a contingency fee, you have the benefit of a complimentary annual review of your assessed value and are billed only when the agent reduces your property taxes. Many property owners appreciate knowing that a performance-based consultant is reviewing their assessed value annually and billing only when he achieves results.

 PRACTICE TIP–Ask your consultant if they invoice for "market value" reductions that do not reduce the assessed value or reduce your property taxes.

Having a tax consultant reviewing your assessed value annually increases the likelihood of achieving reductions in your assessed value for several reasons. First, the agent is more likely to protest the assessed value. Given the pressure of obligations in everyday life, you may or may not focus on a notice of an increase in the assessed value from the appraisal district. Even if you do review it, you may decide that the chance of a reduction is marginal and not worth the time involved. Secondly, the staff appraiser performing the informal hearing has a strong influence on whether there is a reduction in the assessed value. By protesting your assessed value annually, the agent increases the chance of a hearing with a flexible staff appraiser who will reduce the assessed value. Thirdly, the agent is better prepared to compile data and present the protest since the incremental time for one additional case is much less than the time it would take you to prepare for and present the property tax protest.

Finally, and perhaps most importantly, a professional property tax consultant will have an edge over someone who handles a limited number of protests annually. Many tax consultants previously worked at one or more central appraisal districts and are keenly aware of the process and procedures. They understand the nuances involved in the process and what is working during the current year versus what worked last year. Tax consultants often adjust their strategy during the hearing season and will know what strategy will work best in your particular case. Larger tax consultant firms handle more than 10,000 hearings per year and have multiple agents working full time at the appraisal district during the peak season. It is simply not practical for an individual to be able to duplicate the knowledge and experience they have developed while attending property tax hearings one or two days per year.

However, a tax consultant probably doesn't know your property as well as you. Even after educating the consultant, he may not fully understand the quirks and foibles of your property. In the final analysis, you will have to decide whether you want to handle the protest challenge yourself or turn it over to a professional. In some cases, your knowledge about property can compensate for a lack of technical information and knowledge of the staff.

TAX CONSULTING FEE STRUCTURES

Some agents have only one type of fee structure, but most have a variety. *Typical fee structures include flat fees, hourly fees, contingency fees, and hybrid fees.*

A flat fee is an amount charged annually regardless of results. Typically, a flat fee is charged whether the property is protested or not and whether there is any reduction in the assessed value or not. The flat fee is less than would result from a contingency fee in years when there is a large reduction. However, it is obviously higher than the fee resulting from a contingency fee when there is no reduction.

An hourly fee is charged based on the number of hours spent preparing for and presenting the protest, regardless of the results.

A contingency fee or performance fee is based on the tax savings resulting from the tax agent's work. Contingency fees vary, based on the size of the property and the overall size of the account. They are typically based on the first year's tax savings resulting from the difference in the assessed value between the initial notice value and the value obtained through the tax appeal process. There is often a different contingency fee for the administrative hearing process (informal hearing and appraisal review board hearing) and for litigation or judicial appeal. Some agents handle litigation on a contingency basis. However, most agents do not.

A hybrid fee can be a combination of an hourly fee, a flat fee, and a contingency fee. Typically, a hybrid is based on a flat annual fee plus a contingency fee (based on a portion of the annual tax savings).

PERSONAL ISSUES

One final issue to consider is the *personal satisfaction you will gain from successfully reducing your property taxes*. Many property owners find reducing their taxes an exhilarating and gratifying experience. Most forms of taxation are not subject to a tax appeal process. For example, your federal income taxes are determined by completing the forms. You cannot argue about the amount of income or your level of taxation compared to your neighbor. Federal taxes are a more straightforward calculation. **Winning tax relief can be a**

great experience!

You may want to protest your own taxes for a year to see how much work is involved and whether you enjoy the process. If you have the time and desire to handle your own tax appeal, the result can reduce your taxes as well as provide personal satisfaction. Performing the task involved will also help you understand the opportunities in the tax appeal process.

After you have handled your tax appeal once, you'll better understand the time and tasks involved. This will allow you to make an informed judgment whether the work involved is worth the time required or whether a property tax consultant is a better option. In either case, you can reduce your property taxes to the lowest possible level by annually appealing either personally or by using a property tax consultant.

Chapter 23: Business Personal Property

Tangible business personal property (BPP) is taxable in Texas. This includes equipment and inventory. The non-tangible business personal property, such as accounts receivable, goodwill, and proprietary processes, is not taxable for purposes of Texas property taxes.

The central appraisal district for the county where the property is kept when not in use establishes the assessed value for the business personal property. The county will send business owners a rendition form asking them to list their taxable assets. If the information provided by the property tax owner supports a higher assessed value than currently maintained by the appraisal district, the appraisal district will increase the assessed value to the level supported by data provided by the property owner. If the property owner does not render (provide a list, cost basis, and date acquired), the central appraisal district will take its best guess at what the assessed value should be, based on information such as the size of the property where the business is located or the number of employees.

REALITY CHECK ON MARKET VALUE OF
BUSINESS PERSONAL PROPERTY

While updating this book, the writer was involved in shutting the office of a medical professional.

Consider the following FACTS:

Acquisition cost of equipment	$250,000+
Valued rendered in good faith	50,000
First offer to purchase office equipment	2,700
Second offer to purchase equipment	3,500

In addition to only obtaining $3,500 for equipment value at $50,000, it cost about $1,100 to have undesirable furniture, like very large desks, removed.

The Texas Tax Code requires owners of business personal property to render annually. The penalty for not rendering is 10% of the property taxes. The Texas Supreme Court ruled in the fall of 2000 that a central appraisal district may force a property owner to render.

SHOULD YOU RENDER?

If you prepare a rendition form and analyze your property using the same formulas and methodology employed by your local appraisal district, you can ascertain whether filing the rendition would likely increase or decrease your BPP tax liability. If filing the rendition will increase your personal tax liability, you may still wish to file it, particularly if your assessed value is greatly understated and you are concerned about paying back taxes if the appraisal district learns there is omitted property during the next three years. They can assess for back taxes for a three-year period if they realize that there is omitted property that has not been assessed. If the rendition will decrease your assessed value and property taxes, it makes sense to file the rendition before going through the protest process.

The *deadline for filing a rendition* is April 1. Most business personal property owners elect not to render because of the time required to complete the rendition form and because most of the assessed values for BPP are less than the market value of the property.

 PRACTICE TIP – To get a free copy of *What You Need to Know About Personal Property Valuation*, go to https:wwwpoconnor.com/fussiness-and-personal-property-tax/

FILING A BPP PROTEST

The process for filing a BPP protest is the same as filing a real property protest. It must be filed by the later of May 15 or 30 days after the appraisal district sends notice of the assessed value for the current year. The district is required to send notice of the assessed value if it increases by more than $1,000.

PREPARING FOR A BPP PROTEST HEARING

The appraisal district has forms and ratios it employs to calculate the assessed value of business personal property. These are essentially a book value analysis similar to what an accountant would use. The concept is that the equipment loses a certain portion of its value each year as documented on the schedule. This process is also known as straight line depreciation. The appraisal district's form lists the equipment, initial cost, date of acquisition, and the percentage good (i.e., the market value as a percentage of original cost), together with the assessed value for each item or class of items. You can obtain a copy of the form used by the appraisal district to calculate the assessed value and the manual it uses to assign depreciation for each class of assets either at no cost or a nominal cost by calling or visiting the appraisal district.

PRACTICE TIP – If you render based on the appraisal district's suggestion, your BPP taxes are likely to be double the fair value. Render based on market value and NOT on cost and year of acquisition. For more information, go to https:www.poconnor.com/fussiness-and-personal-property-tax/ to get a free copy of *What You Need To Know about Personal Property Valuations.*

To understand the appraisal district's position at the hearing, you will need to perform the analysis they would perform if they had the information regarding your business personal property. The list of business personal property is typically called a **fixed asset listing**.

PRACTICE TIP – Get a free evaluation. If you have a BPP account, call 713-375-4299 for a free evaluation of your potential savings.

After performing the analysis, you may wish to review the effective age for some of the items, the class to which they belong, and whether the appraisal district's depreciation schedule accurately calculates the assessed value. If you do not feel the appraisal district's depreciation table accurately calculates the market value for your property, you may wish to obtain documentation from a third party such as a used-

O'Connor Tax Reduction Experts 713.369.5958

equipment dealer or an appraiser regarding the market value of the equipment.

OTHER BUSINESS PERSONAL PROPERTY (BPP) ISSUES

The effective date for valuation for business personal property is January 1 of each year. If possible, you may wish to plan to decrease inventory prior to that date and to postpone purchases until after January 1. When preparing a BPP assessment analysis, use the fixed asset listing for January 1 of the appropriate year.

Valuation of inventory in bulk may vary from the cost of the inventory. For example, since inventory is valued on January 1, the returns received by a retailer and the merchandise not purchased by the holiday shoppers remain and are valued at cost, using appraisal district methodology. In most cases, the value of this leftover and returned merchandise will be less than its initial cost of acquisition.

Further, business personal property appraisers believe that bulk inventory is worth less than its initial cost due to obsolescence and shrinkage. For example, $1 million worth of jewelry still in inventory purchased at an aggregate cost of $1 million would likely sell for less than $1 million to a person purchasing the business and inventory. The

278

appropriate value for assessment purposes is the price a person purchasing the inventory to continue the business would pay. It is not a liquidation or fire-sale value. Property tax consultants, business appraisers, or business brokers may be able to help you understand the appropriate level of assessment for large levels of inventory.

The market value for some equipment may be different from the book value or the value indicated by the appraisal district's depreciation analysis. Consider the market value of hotel linens after they have been used for one month. Let's suppose they have an effective life of two years. It is clear that they have lost more than 1/24th of their value after being used for one month.

 PRACTICE TIP – The largest potential savings for BPP is not for inventory; it is for the other types of BPP like furniture, equipment, computers, etc.

Computers are another item which will be likely to depreciate more quickly than the appraisal district's schedules. A three-month-old computer may be worth half of its initial cost, yet it may be assigned a three-year depreciation schedule.

The issue for assessment purposes is the market value of the property. In other words, how much money could

you obtain selling the business personal property to a third party? Market value is the appropriate criteria for establishing your assessed value and property taxes, not the value indicated by a depreciation schedule.

Very few BPP accounts are reasonably assessed; most are taxed at double the market value. **If the appraisal district has detailed information on the property (i.e., a fixed asset listing), their valuation methodology will almost certainly overstate the market value of the equipment and inventory.** When large amounts of BPP are involved, resolution of these accounts is a tedious process where accurate valuation often hinges on estimating effective age and remaining economic life and locating comparable sales.

The most important steps in obtaining a reasonable assessed value for business personal property are: 1) deciding whether or not to render and 2) deciding how to render (providing a value or a fixed asset listing). If you provide a fixed asset listing, the appraisal district WILL use their valuation schedule and substantially over-value the property. You then have to decide if the fight to reduce the taxable value is worth the time and expense. It is not unusual for a business personal property appraisal to cost $5,000 to $20,000. The most effective option is to avoid providing the appraisal district information in the form of a fixed asset listing. If you provide a fixed asset listing, it almost guarantees an expensive battle to achieve a reasonable value.

PRACTICE TIP – O'Connor has developed a proprietary model that can determine if we can help you. There is no cost for a free evaluation. Call 713-374-4299. Services can be rendered on a flat fee, a contingency, or a hybrid schedule. BPP services can also be provided on an appraisal only, with appraisal fees attractive relative to the savings.

Chapter 24: Quick Overview Of Protesting Property Taxes For Your House

Time spent protesting property taxes for your house can be a profitable and exhilarating experience. However, the uncertainty of how the process works and what results are achievable intimidates many into not attempting to protest their property taxes. This chapter gives you a quick overview of the steps involved to decide whether to protest, how to prepare for the protest, and how to present your case at the protest hearing.

 PRACTICE TIP – the question of whether to protest is a red herring. The real question is whether to protest yourself or to have an agent do it for you.

EXCESSIVE AND UNEQUAL APPRAISALS

Your first step is to determine whether to protest your property taxes. The two main criteria for protesting your property taxes are an excessive appraisal and an unequal appraisal. Excessive appraisal means that the assessed value determined for your house by the central appraisal district exceeds the market value of your house. Unequal appraisal means the assessed value for your house is inequitable based on either assessment comparables or the median level of appraisal for your house versus other houses in the area.

The timely filing of a notice of protest is a crucial step in the protest process. If the assessed value of your home increased by more than $1,000 from the assessed value set in a prior year, the central appraisal district is required to send you a notice of assessed value. If the assessed value of your home has not increased by at least $1,000, the central appraisal district may or may not send you notice of the assessed value for the current year for your house. The simplest way to file a timely protest is to send notice to the central appraisal district (for the county in which the house is located) no later than May 15. If the envelope containing the notice of protest is postmarked May 15 or earlier, the protest will be considered by the central appraisal district as timely filed. To file a protest, you can either complete a form protesting the value of your property or simply send a letter identifying the property and property owner. You can obtain the protest form by calling your CAD. In either event, it's best to make certain it is filed or mailed no later than May 15.

PREPARING FOR THE TAX HEARING

The next step of the process is to prepare for your property tax hearings. Preparation for the tax hearings will be divided into three sections: 1) gathering and analyzing data, 2) deciding on a plan of attack for the hearings, and 3) final preparation for the hearings.

GATHERING AND ANALYZING DATA

Gathering and analyzing data includes gathering data from the central appraisal district on your house and comparable sales, preparing a GRM (gross revenue multiplier) analysis if your house is a rental property, and preparing an analysis on unequal appraisal.

 PRACTICE TIP–Section 41.461 of the Texas Property Tax Code entitles you to obtain all information the appraisal district will present at the property tax hearing. When you file your protest, it is probably worthwhile to make a request under Code Section 41.461 that the CAD provides a copy of all information it intends to present at the property tax hearing. The cost of this information is capped at $15 for residential properties. (In practice, the actual cost is typically only $1 or $2.)

After you obtain the information the appraisal district may present at the hearing, study all information including the data for your house, the analysis on unequal appraisal (if one

284

is provided), and the comparable sales. The best place to start is with the central appraisal district information on your house. It will probably be presented in a manner that is difficult to understand because so much data is summarized without detailed explanation. Feel free to call the appraisal district and ask its customer service staff to explain the data it has provided. It may be worthwhile to visit the central appraisal district to gain a better understanding of its information for your property. When you contact the central appraisal district by phone or in person, ask questions regarding the data presented in its comparable sales analysis. This information may also be difficult to understand if the format and content are not familiar.

FINDING INACCURATE DATA

One of the simplest methods of obtaining a reduction in your assessed value is to find inaccurate data in the appraisal district's information (called a record card) for your house which overstates the quality or size of improvements or land. Inaccurately recorded data would be helpful at the protest hearing if, for example, your house is reported to have four bedrooms and it has only three. Other examples of inaccurate information are excessive size, the inclusion of a pool which does not exist, not indicating that the property is adjacent to a major freeway or some other undesirable adjoining property, or overstating the quality or condition of the improvements.

PRACTICE TIP – Most appraisal districts have a factor to reduce land value for an adverse land factor. Document any inaccuracies in the CAD's record card for presentation at the protest hearing. If the CAD has the size of your property recorded inaccurately, you may need to request a field check prior to the hearing to allow the district to verify the information independently.

PRACTICE TIP–It is easier to get a field check in November through March than in April through October. This correction should endure permanently, as would the inaccurate information if not corrected. In conclusion, documenting inaccurate record card information for your house which overstates the quality or size of the land or improvements is one of the most direct ways to obtain a reduction in your assessed value.

COMPARABLE SALES

The sales comparison approach is used most prevalently at property tax protest hearings for houses. You should consider the information on comparable sales provided by the appraisal district. In addition, you may also want to call a local appraiser or real-estate agent for information on comparable sales. They may have sales more helpful than those provided by the CAD. In some cases, the CAD may only have 5 to 10 sales for the area near your house. However, in most cases, the appraisal district has perhaps 20 to 200 sales in the area dating back as far as two or three years. Your objective should be to pick 2 to 5 sales which are as similar as possible to your house in quality, size, and location which document excessive value. Using only one sale doesn't make sense unless there is only one applicable sale. Using more than 5 sales is typically not necessary and will be redundant. After narrowing your selection to 2 to 5 sales, prepare a simple summary which arrays information such as address, sales price, sales price per square foot, size (in square feet), and grade or quality. Then decide which of the selected 2 to 5 sales are most meaningful and should receive most emphasis in your presentation.

LIVABLE VERSUS SALABLE; IF YOUR HOUSE WAS BUILT OR SOLD RECENTLY

Several atypical types of data to collect and analyze include the construction cost if the house was built in the last year or two and was built by you (versus constructed by a builder and simply purchased by you) and the closing statement if your house has recently been purchased. If you hire a contractor and/or subcontractors to build your house, document the actual construction cost plus the purchase price of the land (if it has been purchased recently). If the assessed value exceeds the sum of construction cost plus purchase price (or market value) of the land, the central appraisal district will likely reduce your assessed value to the sum of construction cost plus land. It may want to add an allowance for builder's profit. If you recently purchased your house, the central appraisal district will likely be aware of the sale. If the purchase price for your house is less than the assessed value, a copy of the closing statement will likely allow you to reduce the assessed value to the purchase price if it was purchased during the 12 months before January 1 of the tax year in question. In relatively flat markets, the central appraisal district may use the purchase price for more than one year. However, a recent trend in at least one central appraisal district is to time adjust sales prices upward from the point of sale. In a hot market, this may result in a property purchased for $100,000 in March being assessed/taxed at $110,000 for January 1 of the following year, based on an increase of 1 percent per month.

FOR RENT HOUSES

If your house is a rental unit, consider using the gross revenue multiplier or GRM method of valuation. To calculate the value of a house using the GRM method, simply multiply the monthly rental rate times the appropriate GRM factor. This factor is typically 70 to 110. To determine the appropriate GRM factor for the area in which your property is located, you can call or visit your CAD to determine the GRM factor used for the area or call an appraiser or Realtor™. If your house is rented for $500 per month and the appropriate GRM factor for the area is 90, the value will be calculated as follows:

$500 per month x 90 = $45,000

DISCOUNT FOR CONDITION OF A RENTAL HOUSE

Unequal appraisal is the issue that generates the largest amount of frustration for property owners. When property owners review the assessed value for their house and for other houses in the area, they often feel that their house is excessively appraised compared to neighboring houses. Preparing for a protest hearing using unequal appraisal can be as simple as gathering information on 5 or 10 assessment comparables and making adjustments for differences or it can be as complicated as preparing a ratio study. Both of these issues were addressed in detail in Chapter 13.

SUMMARY OF PROTEST OPTIONS

The next step is to decide on a plan of attack for your hearing. Options for requesting a reduction in your assessed value include the following:

> ➤ **Appraisal district information overstates the size or quality of your house**

> ➤ **Sales comparables support a lower assessed value**

> ➤ **Cost of construction is less than the assessed**

value (for recently built houses)

➢ **The recent purchase price is less than assessed value**

➢ **GRM analysis indicates a lower value (used primarily for rent houses)**

➢ **Assessment comparables indicate value should be lowered**

➢ **Ratio study supports a lower value**

After reviewing the above information, decide whether to focus on excessive appraisal or unequal appraisal. However, you may present a protest hearing based on excessive appraisal and unequal appraisal. It is unlikely that all of the above information analysis will support a reduction in assessed value. Select the methods most productive to supporting a lower assessed value for your house and gather documentation to present the information in a concise and meaningful manner. For example, if you are requesting a lower assessed value based on comparable sales, you may want to prepare a summary of the sales comparables you believe are most appropriate for the staff appraiser or appraisal review board to consider with a map of the sales and your house.

 PRACTICE TIP–Photographs of the comparable sales and your house can be persuasive evidence.

The final step in preparing for the protest hearing is to make five copies of all documentation (in case you proceed to the formal or appraisal review board hearing) and to establish target and ARB values. The target value is the opening position in your negotiation. Stated differently, it is the lowest value supported by reasonable evidence. The ARB value should be determined before the informal hearing. The ARB value is the highest acceptable value you will accept at the informal hearing. If you don't obtain an assessed value equal to or less than the ARB value at the informal hearing, you will proceed to the formal or ARB hearing.

ATTEND THE PROTEST HEARINGS

You are now properly prepared for your protest hearing. You should feel comfortable, confident, and ready for the hearing. In fact, if you have done most of the preparation discussed, you will be more prepared than at least 90 percent of individual property owners attending a hearing for their property. There are two steps to the administrative protest hearing process: the informal hearing and formal (ARB) hearing. Call the local appraisal district to determine if you need to show up early for the informal hearing. At most appraisal districts the informal hearing starts at the scheduled time. However, at some appraisal districts, the scheduled time is for the ARB hearing. For example, at Dallas Central Appraisal District, the scheduled time is for the appraisal review board hearing. If you want an informal hearing at Dallas Central Appraisal District, either come at least a day prior to the scheduled hearing or early on the day of the hearing. At Dallas, you do not need an appointment for an informal hearing and they give priority to individual taxpayers. At these appraisal districts, if you want to attend an informal hearing, you need to show up before the scheduled time. The informal hearing is not required for either the property owner or the appraisal district. However, most property tax protests are resolved at the informal hearing level.

INFORMAL HEARING

After arriving for the informal hearing, you may have to wait 15 to 60 minutes before the hearing actually starts. Do not let your frustrations interfere with establishing rapport with your informal hearing appraiser at the beginning of the hearing. He cannot affect the amount of time you have to wait; he cannot affect the overall tax rates set by the city, county, and school; and he cannot affect the quality of government services. However, he can adjust your assessed value at the informal hearing.

Present the information you have prepared and ask the staff appraiser to adjust your assessed value to the target assessed value. Since you have done an excellent job of preparing for the hearing, you won't be focusing on issues such as crime in the neighborhood and taxes that are too high and comparing your increase in assessed value with the increase in market value for houses in the neighborhood. Your presentation will be focused on meaningful information that the appraiser can use to adjust your assessed value.

After presenting your information, **actively listen** to the response from the staff appraiser and ask questions to determine what he is trying to accomplish. In his book *The 7 Habits of Highly Effective People*, Stephen Covey writes, "Seek first to understand, then to be understood." If the appraiser asks a question, he may be trying to help give you an opportunity to present the information which can be used to reduce your assessed value. At most informal hearings the CAD appraiser is delighted to find a quick justification to make an adjustment in the assessed value which satisfies the homeowner and completes the hearing. If appropriate, present additional information followed by a counteroffer after listening to the appraiser's comments and offer.

After negotiating with the staff appraiser at the informal hearing you will need to do one of three things: 1) agree to an acceptable value, 2) decide to take your protest to the ARB (formal) hearing, or 3) decide to sign off if you don't want to spend the time to take the protest to the ARB hearing or if the evidence supports an increase in your assessed value.

FORMAL HEARING

The formal or ARB hearing sounds intimidating, but don't let the name scare you. The ARB hearing procedures are relaxed and informal; the ARB hearing typically lasts only 15 minutes. Those attending the formal hearing include the three ARB panel members, the central appraisal district appraiser (who may be different from the appraiser at the informal hearing), and a hearing clerk at some counties. The formal hearing begins with several administrative processes including oaths by you and the appraisal district appraiser. The ARB members also sign an agreement that they have not discussed the property before the hearing. The next step is to exchange information with the appraisal district appraiser. If you filed a 41.461 request (at least 14 days before the hearing), the appraisal district appraiser may not use any evidence not previously presented to you at the hearing (tax code 41.67). The typical hearing format is as follows:

(1) Oaths

(2) Description of the property by CAD appraiser

(3) Presentation of evidence by the property owner

(4) Questions from ARB members

(5) Cross-examination of the property owner by the appraiser

(6) Presentation of evidence by CAD appraiser

(7)   Questions from ARB members

(8)   Cross-examination of the appraiser by the property owner

(9)   Rebuttal by the property owner

(10) The decision by the ARB members

The ARB panel will render its decision and the hearing will conclude. While the ARB panel members may give a brief explanation of their decision, it is not negotiable after it has been rendered.

FURTHER EVIDENCE OF APPEAL

If you are not satisfied with the value determined at the appraisal review board hearing, you may file a judicial appeal, file for binding arbitration or file an appeal with State Office of Administrative Hearings. However, for most homeowners, a judicial appeal (lawsuit) is not financially feasible due to the cost of legal and expert witness services. If you resolved your protest at the informal hearing, no further avenues of appeal are available.

Chapter 25: Great Property Tax Heist
Of 2018

Hurricane Harvey struck the Texas Gulf Coast in August 2017 causing record destruction–$190 billion. Over 100,000 houses were flooded. 80% of homeowners did not have flood insurance; most don't have money for renovation. Despite record devastation of the Gulf Coast area, many appraisal districts are not attempting to identify which properties flooded. Open record requests sent to the appraisal districts for the most part have yielded meager results. Most appraisal districts are relying on self-reporting. This is simply an abdication of their duty.

Is The Appraisal District Working for You? – Follow the Money!

Appraisal district's budgets can approach $100 million per year per county. And there are over 250 counties in Texas. That is a lot of money. And you ask from whence does the money come to pay the chief appraiser and staff and rent and everything else? It comes from the tax entities, like cities, counties, schools, and municipal utility districts (MUDS), among others.

GOVERNANCE

Since the schools, cities, counties, and MUDs pay the bills of running the appraisal district, it would be reasonable to assume that they have some input in the operation of the appraisal district, right? The answer is yes. Tax entities appoint representatives to be on the appraisal district board of directors. The board of directors has two primary areas of responsibility: 1) select a chief appraiser to serve at their pleasure and 2) approve the budget. In practice, once the board of directors selects a chief appraiser, they generally defer to the direction of the chief appraiser in virtually all matters.

ENTITY MEETING

At least one, and likely many more, appraisal districts hold meetings with representatives of tax entities giving an indication of likely changes in value, typically late or early in the year. Before the current year tax rolls are sent, tax entities are given a preview of the values for the coming year. However, to my knowledge these meetings are not public (I've never been invited to one nor have I seen a public notice of one and I generally have read the local newspaper daily, at least for the last 25 years that I have been in business.)

HURRICANE HARVEY AND HOW APPRAISAL DISTRICTS ARE TREATING AFFECTED PROPERTY OWNERS

Tax Code Section 23 requires appraisal districts to value property at market value using Uniform Standards of Appraisal Practice (USPAP). USPAP requires understanding the properties to appraise them.

WHAT ARE GULF COAST APPRAISAL DISTRICTS DOING?

Most Gulf Coast Appraisal Districts are doing nothing except accepting information from property owners. This is referred to as self-reporting. The author believes that accepting self-reporting only violates USPAP and is an abdication of the appraisal districts responsibility to equally spread the tax load.

PUBLIC KNOWLEDGE OF PROPERTY TAXES

This prompts the idea of doing a survey of the public on property taxes. In reality, the public has very little interest in property taxes except for being able to pay less. Yes, there are those patriots who appeal and show up for the hearing every year and I applaud them. In fact, if you read this, and do your own hearings and have some questions, just call the office and we will be happy to let you meet with an expert at no cost. If you do not understand the appraisal district evidence package or how to get it, call us: 713 290 9700. We have Texas offices in Houston, Dallas, Austin and San Antonio.

CONNECTING THE DOTS

Shocked property owners who still are devastated by the flood from Hurricane Harvey are not going to be focused on property taxes. They will probably not even think about property taxes. Most Gulf Coast appraisal districts are relying only on self-reporting. This means flooded property owners in most counties will likely be taxed at two to three times the market value of their property, if they have not remodeled.

THAT IS FLOODING

In addition, about 70 percent of Harris County was underwater during Hurricane Harvey. That does not mean the house flooded, but the lot flooded part-way to the house.

The Texas seller disclosure notice form requires the seller to disclose material facts. Misrepresentation is subject to triple damages under the Texas Deceptive Practices Act. You really do not want to be sued for misrepresentation under the Deceptive Trade Practice Act (DTPA). The seller's disclosure notice form starts with a reference to the property. The property is NOT just the house. The property is the land; the house is the improvements. If one sold a house on January 1, 2018 (effective date for valuation after Harvey) let's consider the possible consequences:

You disclose that the lot flooded but clearly note that the house did not flood. Some buyers are passing on anything that flooded. The universe of buyers for your house is smaller; perhaps much smaller since Harvey was only 4 months in the past. The author believes a ten percent discount is reasonable in this situation.

You do not disclose that the lot flooded and you sell the property at top of the market since it did not flood! There is no flooding in Houston for 15 years and no one is concerned about silly "land flooding" the prior year.

You do not disclose the lot flooded and you sell the property at top of the market since it did not flood! Regrettably, eight months after the sale, Hurricane Alice strikes causing only half of the damage of Harvey. Unfortunately, (bad news seems to clump), due to a different distribution of rainfall, your former home does flood this time! The buyer is out visiting with the neighbors lamenting his bad luck in buying a house in an area that had never flooded before. The neighbor now tells him about the two near misses in three years. And the neighbor is a lawyer specializing in DTPA claims.

Whether or not you take the chance, the reality is the value is lower.

O'Connor has maps that show the locations of flooding every 4 hours and the wind speeds by location every 15 minutes. It is not difficult to get this information.

The second major issue is that the appraisal districts, who are aware of which properties flooded, are overvaluing the properties. Before explaining the overvaluation, let me give kudos to Roland Altinger, Jason Cunningham and team at Harris County Appraisal District (HCAD) for likely doing the best job of any appraisal district in Texas in identifying which properties flooded. HCAD viewed 200,000 to 300,000 properties and identified those that flooded. Also, kudos to Glen Whitehead and his team at Fort Bend Appraisal District. My understanding is that they are attempting to identify the properties that flooded.

VALUATION

Appraisal districts appear to be valuing property that flooded at 60% to 80% of the pre-flood value. However, our research of 1,350 houses indicates houses that flooded and have not been resold, flooded houses are selling for 35% to 41% of the pre-flood value. The appraisal district values are about **double** the actual market value.

O'Connor estimates that in the 55-county Gulf Coast area the appraisal districts will effectively transfer **$2 billion of wealth** from property owners to tax entities. By not doing their job correctly, Texas appraisal districts will generate **$2 billion more in property taxes** than if they had done their job properly. But then they do work for the tax entities. Enough said?

CHAPTER 26: Final Thoughts

My purpose in writing this book is to help the average Texas resident to become familiar with the entire property tax protest process. From experience, I know that the large corporations are able to hire attorneys and tax consultants to get their taxes lowered. This option is not as readily available to the person whose real property consists of a single-family house and who has no knowledge of the property tax protest process.

Texas property taxes have risen sharply over the last twenty years, at about three times the rate of inflation. This is due to both rising property values and assessment ratios. The assessment ratio is the ratio of the assessed value divided by the market value.

It is this situation which compelled me to write this book. I hope the satisfaction you derive from applying the principles outlined here in order to win property tax relief is as great as mine is as I work with thousands of people to ensure that their property is equitably taxed.

–Patrick C. O'Connor

P.S. YOU can spend your money better than the government.

To view the full list of the Central Appraisal Districts of Texas and their information, visit:

bit.ly/TxCADList

Special Offer to purchasers of

"Cut Your Texas Property Taxes"

Get a FREE evaluation to determine if you are being
overtaxed with our Texas Fairness Checker

Go to www.CutMyTaxes.com

Index

A

accounts receivable, 84, 273

amortization, 188

apartments, 56, 168-169, 173, 182, 184, 188, 191, 207, 209, 213

appeals, *see* judicial appeals

appraisal districts, 14, 18, 20-22, 32-34, 39, 43, 47-56, 80, 89, 93, 95, 104-109, 117-119, 123-127, 130-131, 141, 151, 193, 198, 212, 217, 220, 226-228, 230-233, 243, 247, 267-268, 285, 290, 295-300, 303

and number of appraisals, 51-52, 226

appraisal methods, 140-141

see also cost approach, iv, 24-25, 42, 48-50, 136, 140, 164-168,. 179, 200, 208, 210-213, 232, 237

see income approach to appraising real estate,

sales comparison approach, 42, 51, 164-167, 169, 172-173, 175-176, 180, 200, 216, 219, 224, 285

appraisal records, 22, 78, 87, 99-101

accuracy of, 22, 32, 34, 43, 50, 227, 230, 263

correction of, 91

appraisal review boards (ARB), 22, 34-36, 55, 88-89, 124-125, 214, 218, 220, 231, 133

and informal appraiser, 122, 243-244, 248, 250-251

appraisers,18-21, 33, 40, 42, 49-54, 117, 119, 121-

external depreciation, 107

external obsolescence, 106-107, 108

E

economic development groups, 66

economic life, 184, 188, 202-204, 279

economic obsolescence, 48

effective age, 53-54, 203-204, 276, 279

effective gross income, 51, 183,186, 191

(EGIM), 51

effective tax rates, 4

elderly persons, 244

exemptions for, iii, vi, 1, 14, 16, 58, 61, 64, 66-68,

73, 75-78, 144

entrepreneurial profit,166, 201, 210

equipment, 67-68, 88, 272-

future income, 91

F

failure to give notice, 43

fall-back positions, 124, 126, 158

farm products exemptions, 34

farming exemptions, 34

federal exemptions, 33

Federation of Women's

, 41, 125, 135, 262

for paying taxes, 1, 18, 70, 72, 75, 84-85, 134, 274

G

garages, 84-85

general exemptions, 32

general operating
expenses,

see operating expenses

goodwill, 147

government exemptions,
33

grid analysis, 85-86

gross income multiplier,
99

gross rent multiplier
(GRM), 153, 156,

157

gross revenue multipliers
(GRM), 26, 157

275, 277-279

equity protests, 77, 201,
251

H

handicapped
exemptions, 14-15

Harris County Appraisal
District, 14, 23, 28, 30,
32, 44, 119, 127, 133,
157, 193, 247, 300

hearings, 33, 35, 40-41,
46, 89, 95, 103, 112,
114-119, 122, 124, 126,
132, 137, 164-167, 179,
198-201, 212-214, 220,
228, 246-249, 254, 263-
260, 282, 290, 292, 294,
298

appraisal review
boards, 118, 127-128,
254, 256

informal hearings,
220, 247, 292

protest hearings , 97,
133, 200, 205, 212, 266,
285, 290

highest and best use

For All of Your Texas Property Tax Needs

O'Connor

2200 North Loop West, Suite 200

Houston, TX 77018

(713) 290-9700

1-833-CUT-MY-TAXES

www.CutMyTaxes.com